CUT-OUTS AND CUT-UPS
A Lesbian Activity Book

Elizabeth Dean, Linda Wells, and Andrea Curran

Illustrations By Ginger Brown

New Victoria Publishers
Norwich, Vermont

© 1989 by Elizabeth Dean, Linda Wells, and Andrea Curran
All rights reserved

Library of Congress catalog card number 89-060947
ISBN 0-934678-20-0

Published by New Victoria Publishers
P.O. Box 27 Norwich, Vermont

DISCLAIMER

The characters portrayed in this book, while they may greatly resemble your current lover, a roommate, the pitcher on your softball team, an ex-lover, or any member of the lesbian community, are fictitious. Any resemblance to a living or deceased person, or to a person you would like to be either living or deceased, is purely coincidental.

ACKNOWLEDGEMENTS

The authors wish to acknowledge the talented artistry of Ginger Brown, especially in helping to give the dykes portrayed in this book the necessary third *dimension.*

The authors would like to thank Claudia Lamperti at New Victoria Publishers for believing in this project from the start and for showing them what fun there can be in lesbian humor.

Elizabeth Dean dedicates this book to the main character in her book *As the Road Curves*, Ramsey Sears, who was quite miffed to find her author working on another book that didn't involve her in any way, shape, or form. When Ramsey read the manuscript, however, she did comment gruffly that the book seemed okay, "if you like that sort of thing."

Linda Wells would like to acknowledge the help of her local lesbian community, WOBBLES (West of Boston Lesbians), and The Book Club for unwittingly providing the inspiration for the characters in this book. She dedicates this book to them, in the hopes that they will forgive her.

Andrea Curran dedicates this book to Gail and to Amy.

AUTHORS' BIOGRAPHIES

Elizabeth Dean is a frustrated stand-up comedienne who believes her best jokes are the ones she happens to think of when no one else is around. When these jokes are explained at a later date to friends, the usual feedback she receives is, "Stick to writing. So far you haven't fucked that up too badly." She's the author of *As the Road Curves*.

Linda Wells is a nice kid from a small town who is writing phobic and who decided long ago that the only reasons she would participate in the writing of a book would be if it had lots of pretty pictures, made people laugh, and didn't take itself (or anyone else) too seriously.

Andrea Curran thinks of herself primarily as a writer of unpublished unrequited love poems. Her previous literary achievements consist of writing occasional humorous articles for a small-town newspaper as well as editing and proofreading grant proposals, her friends' term papers, and the local lesbian newsletter. Otherwise, this distinguished author occupies herself working in a small public library and cleaning houses.

INTRODUCTION

When the three of us first got together to discuss writing this book, we decided that what we really wanted to work toward was a much-needed humorous look at lesbians, a book that could provide entertainment while poking fun at ourselves in the process, and yet not offend anyone (or at least offend everyone equally). We realized that, being suburban WASP lesbians, we could not speak for every woman of the gay persuasion.

For example, we are not lesbians of color, nor are we Jewish. We do not view life as a city lesbian might, although we do occasionally make expeditions to Boston or Cambridge. We cannot speak for differently-abled lesbians. We haven't a clue what it might be like to be tall and/or overweight lesbians. And we have no understanding whatsoever of the special issues facing red-headed or left-handed lesbians.

So here is our book, written from the perspective of three white, Anglo-Saxon, Protestant, suburban, brown-haired, right-handed lesbians of average height and build who try to find humor, fun, and games wherever we can.

Table of Contents

Connect the Dykes	1
Mad Women's Libs	10
Fill in the Bubbles	19
Girl Groups	22
What's Wrong with this Picture?	24
Word Searches	25
Crystal Clear	31
Women of the Seventies	33
Sister Colleges	35
Rap Group	36
To a Tee	37
Acrostics	38
Classic Vowels	43
Jumbles	44
Numberless	48
More Fill in the Bubbles	54
Crosswords	56
More Fill in the Bubbles	62
Lesbian Book of Questions	63
Locate the Lesbian	66
Let's be Honest Girls	67
Lesbian Zodiac	69
Not so Trivia Herstory	82
Cut Outs	84
Answers	115

CONNECT THE DYKES

The object of this exercise is to test your ability to identify and distinguish between different (stereo)types of lesbians. We have provided you with eight pictures of various kinds of lesbians. Your mission (should you choose to accept it) is to match an item from each category with the pictures.

After you have completed the exercise, you can further amuse yourself by identifying which type you or your friends resemble the most. Or you can study the various types to help you decide which clothing or hairstyles are most appropriate for going out on the town or to work. You can also use the exercise as an aid in locating certain kinds of lesbians and knowing what to say to them once you have found them. This exercise is designed to be informative as well as fun. Answers on pages 83-111

The descriptions of categories are on pages: 5-9
1) Identification—page 5
2) Description—pages 5-6
3) Accoutrements—page 7
4) Habitat— page 7
5) Transportation—page 8
6) Common expressions—page 8
7) Last book read—pages 8-9
8) Heroine—page 9
9) Social group or professional affiliation—page 9

1)___ Identification
2)___ Description
3)___ Accoutrements
4)___ Habitat
5)___ Transportation
6)___ Common expressions
7)___ Last book read
8)___ Heroine
9)___ Social group or professional affiliation

1

1)___ Identification
2)___ Description
3)___ Accoutrements
4)___ Habitat
5)___ Transportation
6)___ Common expressions
7)___ Last book read
8)___ Heroine
9)___ Social group or professional affiliation

1)___ Identification
2)___ Description
3)___ Accoutrements
4)___ Habitat
5)___ Transportation
6)___ Common expressions
7)___ Last book read
8)___ Heroine
9)___ Social group or professional affiliation

1) ___ Identification
2) ___ Description
3) ___ Accoutrements
4) ___ Habitat
5) ___ Transportation
6) ___ Common expressions
7) ___ Last book read
8) ___ Heroine
9) ___ Social group or professional affiliation

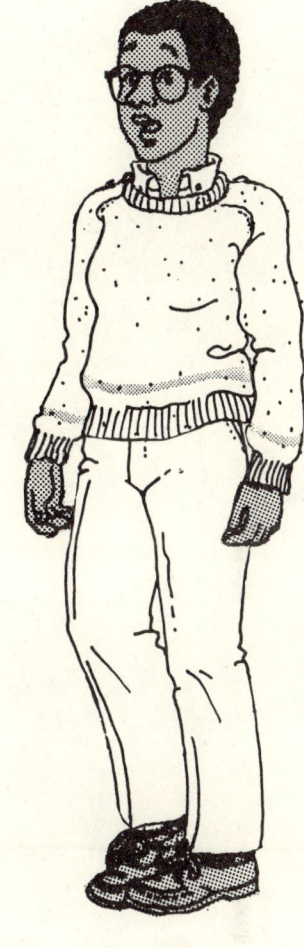

1) ___ Identification
2) ___ Description
3) ___ Accoutrements
4) ___ Habitat
5) ___ Transportation
6) ___ Common expressions
7) ___ Last book read
8) ___ Heroine
9) ___ Social group or professional affiliation

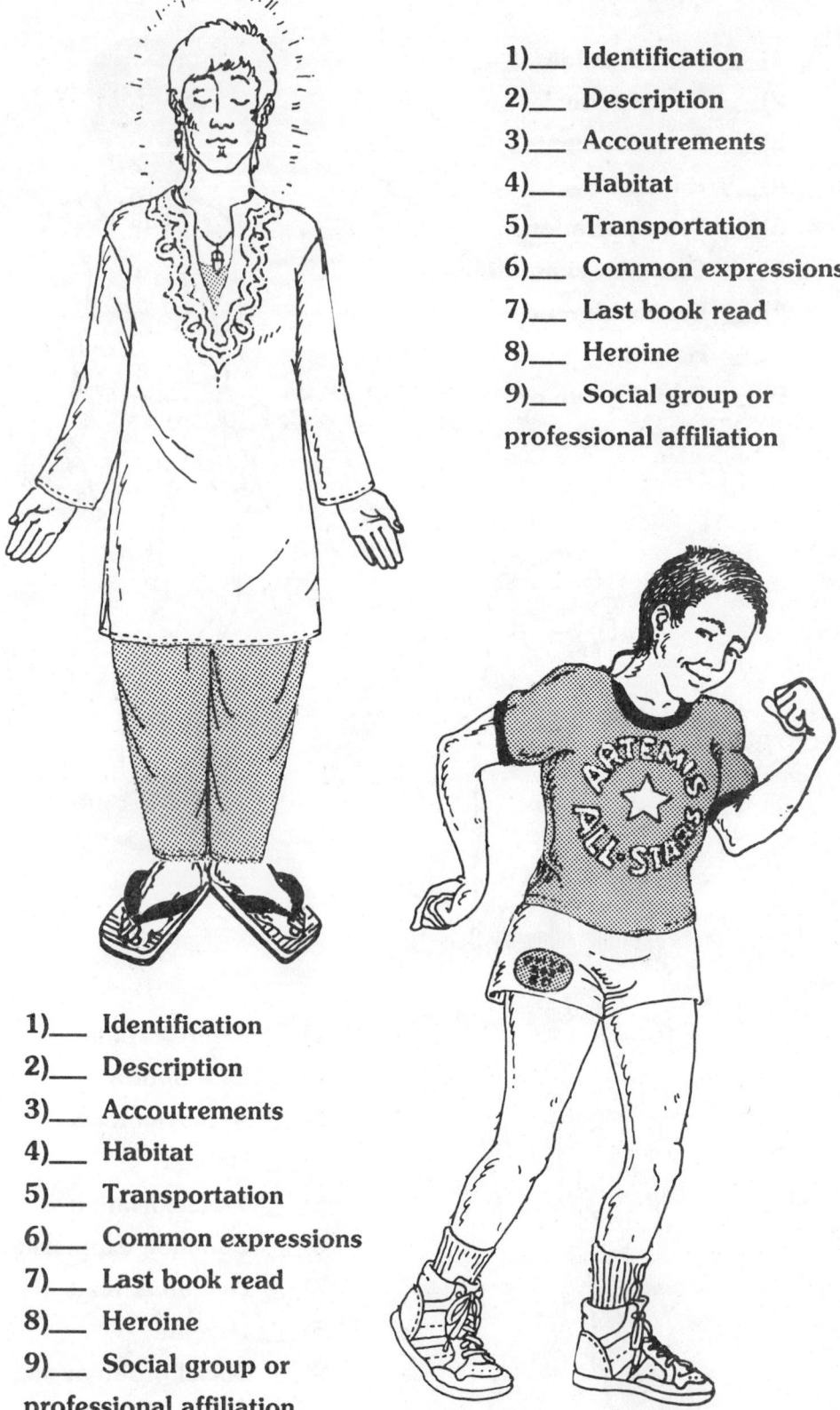

1)___ Identification
2)___ Description
3)___ Accoutrements
4)___ Habitat
5)___ Transportation
6)___ Common expressions
7)___ Last book read
8)___ Heroine
9)___ Social group or professional affiliation

1)___ Identification
2)___ Description
3)___ Accoutrements
4)___ Habitat
5)___ Transportation
6)___ Common expressions
7)___ Last book read
8)___ Heroine
9)___ Social group or professional affiliation

1)___ Identification
2)___ Description
3)___ Accoutrements
4)___ Habitat
5)___ Transportation
6)___ Common expressions
7)___ Last book read
8)___ Heroine
9)___ Social group or professional affiliation

1) Identification—Label that Lesbian

A) Don Juanita, B) The Jock, C) Social Worker, D) Intellegentsia, E) Baby Dyke, F) Timberdyke, G) Earth Crunchy, H) Spacey Stacey

2) Description

A) Her head tilted empathically to one side and her long hair loose, demonstrating relaxed receptivity, she is inexpensively stylish in a funky sort of way. Her accessories include a kerchief around her neck, dangling earrings, and bangle bracelets. She wears oversized shirts tied with a sash, free flowing long skirts, wool socks, and Birkenstock sandals.

B) This young innocent is readily identified by her preppy-like boyish appearance, complete with button-down collar, pullover sweater, chinos and deck shoes. She looks at her newly-discovered world with wide-eyed wonderment while keeping herself tightly under wraps.

C) She wears her hair long and braided because it would be unnatural to cut it. She has an Ivory Girl face, complete with clear skin and big eyes that take in everything. This lesbian marches to the beat of a different drummer, usually a slow one. Everything, including speech, is slowly and carefully considered. She wears all-natural fibers, from her cotton shirt and denim overalls to her woolen socks slipped into leather clogs.

D) She's a smooth operator, dressed to the nines at every social occasion. Her moussed hair is brushed back from her face for that lean and hungry look. She adorns herself with long dangling earrings, a bracelet or two, and gold chains around her neck. She wears a high-necked silk shirt under her double-breasted evening jacket. Her stylish black pleated pants taper at the bottom over her shiny black pointed leather shoes.

E) The self-proclaimed intellectual elite of the lesbian community, she controls her life through her "superior" reasoning powers and her ability to criticize everyone and everything. Her dress is conservative, usually well coordinated clothes from a discount department store. Social wear consists of a cotton blouse under a sweater, corduroys usually a bit too short, argyle socks, and sensible shoes. Formal wear would include a blazer.

F) She wears her hair short so that she can always keep her eye on the ball. She is ready for action in her muscle-revealing tight tee-shirt tucked into her fashionable sweat pants. She is usually wearing white sweat socks in her all-purpose cleats. With a happily competitive outlook, she's up for any game anytime.

G) Loose-fitting clothes (so as not to impede the flow of spiritual energy) and a proliferation of crystals hanging from various parts of her body are characteristics of this lesbian. Her clothes mirror her eclectic spiritual practice: multicolored silk pants from Africa, a large bandana in imitation of an Indian serape for a top, and a turban (just for the impact). She is easily recognized by her starry-eyed expression, an aura of serenity, and a perpetual "OM" on her lips.

H) This strong and sturdy woman is usually found wearing a worn flannel shirt, tan steel-toed boots with woolen socks rolled over the tops, old jeans with holes at the knees exposing red long underwear, and a visored cap with John Deere imprinted on the front. Her face is perpetually tanned and weathered, with squint lines around her eyes from looking into the sun. She has a satisfied look on her face from having created things with her own hands.

3) Accoutrements

A) A calendar listing from the regional gay newspaper.

B) Chainsaw optional.

C) Incense, feathers, and an amulet filled with special crystals and stones.

D) Softball glove, bat, or any sports equipment in season.

E) She is often seen reaching for GORP (grains, oats, raisins and peanuts) in her pocket and usually carrying around a cup of hot herbal tea.

F) She is armed with a little black book and a cigarette lighter.

G) A proverbial date book and a portable clock.

H) Always prepared with book, pens, notebooks and often computer paper.

4) Habitat

A) Softball fields, basketball courts, golf courses, tennis courts, and grouped en masse in front of any televised sporting event.

B) This type of lesbian used to be found almost exclusively at John Denver concerts but now she is everywhere: gardens, camping areas, health food stores, weaving classes, and massage centers.

C) She is found on college campuses, Cris Williamson concerts, or at any women's event anywhere.

D) She is most often found at lectures, seminars, workshops (any place where CEUs can be obtained), and in the Juvenile Courts.

E) When not in the woods, this woman can be found in hardware or feed and grain stores early on a Saturday morning. She is also likely to be spotted anywhere that tractors or other large earth-moving equipment are found.

F) This type of lesbian's social highlight is the monthly book club, where she has the opportunity to flex her intellectual biceps and, with her peers, reveal her profound insights into other people's writing.

G) She is found in bars, at softball games, potlucks, dances-- basically anyplace where lesbians are to be cruised (no event is too large or too small for a Cassanova lesbian).

H) Her habitat includes metaphysical bookstores, retreats, and workshops entitled How To Be A Channel Of Love For The Universe While Attaining Personal and Planetary Prosperity.

5) Transportation

A) Any car that has been carefully researched and comparison priced so that the best value for the least money has been achieved.

B) A red sports car (or at least the desire for one).

C) An American made pick-up truck, battered but loved.

D) Her parents' car complete with college stickers, graduation tassels, and assorted toys on the dashboard.

E) A small station wagon, large enough to carry athletic gear, yet compact enough to look sporty.

F) An old VW Squareback, large enough to carry camping or gardening gear or for sleeping in while traveling.

G) She levitates.

H) She drives an economical yet functional Japanese car complete with all the amenities.

6) Common Expressions

A) "Would you like some more herbal tea? " "What was I saying?"

B) The single most common word proclaimed by her is "But." As in, "I agree with you whole-heartedly but.... I know you are an expert in this field but...." Whatever the conversation, you can rest assured she will stick her "but" into it.

C) The words most often out of her mouth are, "How do you feel about that?" And, "Thank you for sharing that with me."

D) "Diamonds are a girl's best friend."

E) With the zealousness of a new convert, she proclaims sixties feminist rhetoric as her own.

F) "Have we met before? Your eyes are so intense! What sign are you? I usually don't act this way with people I've just met, but...."

G) Besides terse comments about the weather, she is not likely to engage in idle conversation, especially while the sun is still up.

H) Besides her Mantra she often can be heard uttering phrases like, "Mercury is in retrograde, that's why I'm screwing up. I love your crown chakra halo."

7) Last Book Read

A) The Time-Life Series on *How To Build Your Own Outhouse*

B) She rarely reads and when she does it is exclusively about sports; athletes' autobiographies, the sports pages of the newspaper, and sports listings in the *TV Guide*.

C) *Lesbian Psychologies* edited by the Boston Lesbian Psychologies Collective

D) Any book by Shirley MacLaine

E) The A-L section of the local library, alphabetically

F) *Rubyfruit Jungle*, by Rita Mae Brown, because it is the only lesbian book she knows about.

G) *The Foxfire* books, and the *Whole Earth Catalogue;* it is possible she has read J.R.R. Tolkien's trilogy again.

H) *Lesbian Sex* and *Lesbian Passion*, by JoAnn Loulan, *Pleasures*, by Lonnie Barbach, *The Joy Of Lesbian Sex*, by Emily l. Sisley and Bertha Harris. ANYTHING, including the *Dictionary* and the *Bible*, as long as there is sex in it.

8) Her Heroine is...

A) Shirley MacLaine

B) Annie Oakley and the spirit of the frontier women

C) Adelle Davis

D) Martina, Nancy Leiberman, Billie Jean King, and her high school gym teacher

E) The heroine in *Rubyfruit Jungle*, by Rita Mae Brown

F) Carol Gilligan, Jean Baker Miller, and all the blessed beings at the Stone Center.

G) Patricia Charboneau, star of *Desert Hearts*.

H) She does not have a heroine because she finds fault with everyone.

9) Social Group or Professional Affiliation

A) She is involved in any group where there is potential for becoming involved with any of the group's members.

B) 25 and under lesbian rap groups

C) Food co-ops, clothing co-ops, communal gardens, shared homes, covens and country dances

D) A member of any group exploring whatever metaphysical topic is currently in vogue

E) She joins support groups for lesbian therapists who are survivors of traditional clinical practice.

F) The book club or any organization where her intellectual and critical skills can be utilized

G) Wilderness Women of Washington County

H) Softball teams, hockey teams, basketball teams, touch football teams, and, when desperate, golf and bowling leagues

Mad Women's Libs

Rules:

This is a great party game, guaranteed to introduce an element of silliness to any gathering. One person asks the other group members for the parts of speech indicated and writes them in the spaces provided. Then the completed story is read back to the group accompanied, of course, by gales of laughter. Note: There are no "right" answers!

Breaking Up is Hard to Do

_____ had just been dumped by her lover, who had left her for
woman's name

a(n) _____ woman. Everywhere she looked, she saw reminders of
     adjective

her ex: the _____ hanging on the wall, the _____ they
    plural noun   plural noun

had bought together, the _____ they had shared. She remembered
                              noun

the _____ trip they had taken to _____
    adjective   place

and the time they had _____ together. She couldn't bear
                    past tense verb

to _____ their _____ tapes any more.
  verb   female singer

She remembered how her ex used to _____ while
                                   verb

_____ her _____. And how many
ing verb   noun

times her ex's _____ had kept her _____. Come
        ing verb   adjective

to think of it, she was better off alone.

Mad Women's Libs

Lesbian Astrology

It is important to know how a lesbian's astrological sign can influence her behavior. An Aries lesbian is fiery and _____ (adjective), while a Taurus is _____ (adjective) and down to earth. Geminis can never decide if they are _____ (plural noun) or _____ (plural noun), and Cancers tend to be emotionally _____ (adjective). Leos are self-confident and like to _____ (verb), while Virgo lesbians may be artistic or even _____ (adjective). And Libras are intellectual and _____ (adjective). One should try to avoid Scorpio lesbians, who are only interested in sex and _____ (plural noun). Sagittarians are hard to live with because they are _____ (adjective) and Capricorns are stable but _____ (adjective). Eccentric Aquarians tend to _____ (verb) other people and there is something fishy and _____ (adjective) about a Pisces lesbian. Remember, astrology is always _____ (adjective).

Mad Women's Libs

Concert

Have you ever been to a _____(female singer)_____ concert? She's the most _____(adjective)_____ performer I've ever seen. Her _____(adjective)_____ songs are enough to break your _____(noun)_____. Her _____(adjective)_____ tunes make everyone want to get up and _____(verb)_____. The audiences are always interesting to look at too: Many women have _____(adjective)_____ hair and _____(adjective)_____ pants. Some have _____(plural noun)_____ all over their bodies. In the backup band, the _____(noun)_____ always sounds _____(adjective)_____ and the bass player is really _____(adjective)_____. So take your _____(noun)_____ to one of these concerts. I guarantee you'll have a really _____(adjective)_____ time.

Doris Clitoris's Etiquette Rule # 1

When going to bed with another for the first time since your long-term relationship has ended, *do not* say to her, "Why don't you sleep on this side of the bed. It is ...was...always her side," and then burst into tears. This is not the way to make a good first impression!

Mad Women's Libs

Lesbians and Their Pets

Have you ever noticed how much lesbians and their pets have in common? For example, an outdoorsy-type _____ lesbian is most
                                                          adjective
likely to own a(an) _____ Laborador Retriever, while
                        adjective
an intellectual lesbian probably keeps company with at least _____
                                                                number
_____ cats. Jocks tend to have athletic and muscular _____
   adjective   noun(s)
and sedentary lesbians like _____ pets. Poodles are
                                adjective
common pets for Baby Dykes. Most _____ lesbians prefer
                                     adjective
pets who will _____ and _____. So if you're thinking
               verb   verb
about getting a pet, make sure it corresponds to your _____
                                                         adjective
lifestyle.

Doris Clitoris's Etiquette Rule # 2
When seating lovers and ex-lovers at a dinner party, always put current lovers across the table from each other, within kicking distance.

Mad Women's Libs

Don Juanita in the Bar

I was sitting alone at a (an) _____ table, nursing my glass of
                                          adjective

_____, when she walked in the door. She was _____.
     liquid   adjective

Her _____ hair was styled beautifully, her silk shirt clung
        adjective

_____ to her well-developed breasts, and her _____
   adverb   adjective

pants left nothing to the imagination. She walked _____
                                                                                adverb

up to me. "Here," she said, "allow me to light your _____."
                                                                                   noun

"But I don't _____," I protested. "Then let's dance," she said.
                    verb

We danced all night, and before she took me home she said, "I've been

looking for a _____ like you all my life."
                 noun

Doris Clitoris's Etiquette Rule # 3
Proper spiking of the hair is best accomplished if the proportion of gel to hair is fifty-fifty. To check if you have used the right amount, cover the top of your head with a softball glove for thirty seconds. Remove the glove. Toss a softball into your glove. Hold the glove upside down. If the ball does not fall out of the glove, you have used the right amount of gel on your hair

Mad Women's Libs

Degaying the Apartment

Here are some _____ tips for what to do when your
                        adjective

parents come to visit and you and your lover aren't out to them. First, tell

them that your lover is really your _____ and doesn't actually
                                          noun

_____ with you all the time. Convert your _____ into a
   verb   room

_____ by putting a _____ into it. Replace the pictures of
   noun   noun

_____ women with ones that are more _____
   adjective   adjective

and likely to inspire parental approval. Remove all lesbian literature from

your bookcase and substitute books about _____ and _____
                                            plural noun   plural noun

instead. Tell them your _____ albums are really _____
                         lesbian singer   adjective

music. If all this doesn't work, you could always tell them the truth.

Doris Clitoris's Etiquette Rule # 4

If during lovemaking, your soft contact lenses become dry, disguise your rapid eye blinking as flirtatious winks and your squinting and eye rolling as reactions to your partner's touch. You might moan, "This is the most intense sex I've ever had," to further validate your strange facial expressions. Then a few minutes after orgasm you may excuse yourself, grope your way into the bathroom, and plop rewetting solution into your eyes.

The Personal Ad

Professional _____ lesbian seeks _____ bisexual
             adjective   adjective

between the ages of _____ and _____ to share similar interests. I enjoy
                   number   number

_____ walks in the moonlight, quiet evenings in front of the
   adjective

_____, listening to _____ albums, and eating _____.
  noun   female singer   plural noun

I prefer that you don't smoke _____ or drink _____. I am
                                   noun   noun

eventually looking for a(n) _____ relationship, but for now I
                             adjective

will settle for _____ times. If you're the _____
              adjective   noun

for me, write soon. I'm _____ awaiting your reply.
                           adverb

Doris Clitoris's Etiquette Rule # 5

Never tell a lover that the reason you're holding onto receipts for items purchased together is, "just in case we break up." Use safe excuses such as: "I'm doing this for tax purposes," "My accountant is soooo finicky," or "I wrote a client's number on the back."

Mad Women's Libs

The Heavy Date

After the movie, _____ (woman's name) invited _____ (woman's name) back to her house. They sat together on the _____ (noun) for a while, listening to a _____ (female singer) album and holding _____ (plural noun). Eventually, they made their way to the _____ (noun), where they _____ (past tense verb) each other's _____ (plural noun). Soon both women were _____ (verb)ing each other's _____ (noun).

"_____ (exclamation)," sighed one. "_____ (exclamation)," screamed the other. When they came (together of course), they sounded like two _____ (plural noun) mating. "That was the best _____ (noun) I've ever had," they agreed.

Doris Clitoris's Etiquette Rule # 6

Never try to dance at a party on shag carpeting. The chances that you will lose your balance and fall face-first into the veggie dip platter are higher than if you sat on the floor and played 'Pictionary.'

Mad Women's Libs

Potluck

The most common lesbian social event is the _____ potluck,
adjective

in which women meet in a(n) _____ setting and bring their
adjective

favorite _____ dish. Some lesbians are _____ and will
adjective   plural noun

eat only _____. Others are vegetarians and can be counted
plural noun

on to bring _____ casseroles. Some lesbians have a real sweet
adjective

tooth and bake fancy _____. Some don't like to cook and
plural noun

bring _____ and cheese. But many lesbians are omnivorous and
plural noun

bring platters of _____ or _____. Even though the
plural noun   plural noun

potluck is a(n) _____ lesbian social event, socializing is always
adjective

secondary to _____.
ing verb

Fill In The Bubbles

The following game is one that we think is more fun shared, but since many of you may be reading this book alone, we'd like to give you a chance to share the fun with other lesbians. Here's how: What follows are cartoons with empty thought and word bubbles so that you can fill them in with your own clever comments. If you want to share, send us your contribution and, if we think it's funny too, we'll print the completed cartoon in our next book. Finalists will also be eligible for the grand prize of a date with Elizabeth Dean. A confirmed Don Juanita, Jock, and Earth Crunchy kinda gal. (She would like you to send a photo and phone number, too!)

Send your entries before Sept. 1, 1990 to Fill-in-the-Bubble Contest
New Victoria Publishers, P.O. Box 27, Norwich, Vermont 05055

Fill In The Bubbles

Fill In The Bubbles

Girl Groups

Listed below are the titles of 20 popular songs from female singers and women's groups popular in the 1960s and 1970s—but with some challenging aspects. The song titles are scrambled. The first word of each title is in column 1. Somewhere in column 2 is the second word of the title. Somewhere in column 3 is the third word, and so on. Correctly identify all 20 titles, then try to guess the artists for each of the titles.

Answers are on page—115

1st word	2nd word	3rd word	4th word	5th word	6th word
Leader	a	Rebel	Me	Love	Forget
My	Turn	Round	Him	Can't	Bad
Sure	Go	Fine	Cry	Roses	
My	of	Follow	the	So	
Soldier	the	to	You		
He's	Guy	the	Kiss		
Then	Get	Back	Him		
Proud	of	Boy	I		
Johnny	Boyfriend's	Kissed	Pack		
Bobby's	in	Postman			
It's	a	Boy			
Johnny	He	Angry			
Kind	Mary	His			
Sally	Boy	Fool			
He's	So	Love			
I	Will				
Judy's	Mr.				
Please	Wanna				
I	Angel				
He's	Girl				

List
Song Titles   **Artists**

___

GAY, GAY, GAY
There are many words that rhyme with GAY. How many can you think of?

3-letter words	4-letter words	5-letter words	6-letter words

What's wrong with this picture?

Answers on page—115

#1 WORD SEARCH —PEOPLE LIKE US

See if you can locate all the words in the following puzzles. You will find them horizontal, vertical, or diagonal, and reading either forwards or backwards.
Answers on page— 116

```
N I U Y V P N G J L Y G T V K D N S B T B B X E S
U F V M U M A M T F T T L Z S F T W R A N R L M B
V D F X A Y N X E B P E A B Y P D E Q L W U P S Q
N V E W W I G A S U A D E E O F V Y B L Q G Y O W
R K Y O C W D A I F N K C E F O B D K F Y B I Y G
D N M G B G J E K B Y K Y N L S O A O E J A T Q S
O A M N J O C K N D S L R H R W W T N U L H M R K
N I I I P D C R O N E E U T R B H E S X Y I E G S
N B B C V D R I N T E L L E G E N T S I A H N U L
A S P A C E Y S T A C Y K K R L F E H L T V E G B
J E W L T S L S Q E D R D M C R A O K O L K O U V
U L G O B S P N K A O N O H I I M I M Y I D T Q C
A W N S M I E Y L W K T E E J O T N C L D C O I Y
N R S Y N E D A L P H Y N I S S A S E O H Y T C O
I M E S J R N A R E Z D X E R I W L P Y S O B L S
T G T T E S I L R T S R X K B F P E F I R O D A H
A E E B S C P S O P H U L S X O L E E E L M M C B
R P M H O I S H F V A C E K E Z M R O T A L T O R
M I M S N G S C I L I L R P P M M M I I H U B Z H
T W E Z F G T T O I E N G U E L O G D G B E F O T
M B F M A V L I X K H S G X N H B Y H P G D A E R
B J R Y A K U W U E F Q Y X A C H P L A X P O R S
U S R Q S I D V J K I A K H R O H U F J G F Q G T
V E G C N I D O G H J A T V V D N Y C B Z T E O W
B Z T K V B Z H F E M M E Y B U T C H W R U B K T
```

BABYDYKE
BUTCHYFEMME
DONNAJUANITA
DYKELING
FEMME
GAY
GIRLFRIEND
HAG
HOMOSEXUAL
INTELLEGENTSIA
JUSTFRIENDS
LESBIAN
LIPSTICKLESBIAN
MAIN
OLDMAID
PEOPLELIKEUS
SISTER
SPACEYSTACY
SWEETHEART
WITCH
BUTCH
CRONE
DYKE
EARTHCRUNCHY
FEMMEYBUTCH
GAYWOMAN
GODDESS
HOMOEROTIC
HOMOSOCIAL
JOCK
LADY
LESBIANMOTHERS
LOVER
MAIDEN
OTHERMOTHERS
SELF
SOCIALWORKER
SPINSTER
TIMBERDYKE
WOMENLOVING

25

#2 WORD SEARCH— ANDY'S

Answers on page—116

```
J L U J K G J L I A D W Y P L G C F C F J C K H C
R P H W Z X Z Y D B O K N E L P P I N R Z G J W J
I T P O H K T T Y R R C W S I W H B B P Y X B U K
R F S Q V M R Y X X P J J C A A X L E A O N A M Z
V E P F O K E Q F F L Y W W D D T F U D I D S Q P
T N H Z K E I O S J O B D S O L Y R X L M A T Y X
R O T T P H L D N V J R F A L X A Q C B H W E T F
D C N F A P W L A T R U C K H B D O O X Y P R T B
A W E G N E I I E L J F A U Y S M L Z A I L B M D
S A X L U Z L D J C K X G A I I Q A D C D L A T S
X R N S C E M M E F Y R G S N O Y V P Y Q A B P Y
N L T X L Y D K U Y W Z T G N L Z E W F C B Y V D
R E G N I F C Z L P D E O E Y C V N X N V T Y L L
B R E A S T Q R B V R U L J Q Y U D S S T E K L C
L Y Z A L J K B O H T A M O Q H Z E S S I K L A P
U I R D Y Z F F O T M M B C T K Z R C X G S O B L
Z B C O C F F O V E O W M K T W C L K X Q A V T D
A Q K K T T D B F Q L M O O K U E U J E A B E F S
L E S B I A N S T O O B R M U R O F L N X S R O I
P D A E A Z R M R H Q E Y Z A T B T I T U U O S R
N A O T A X C B H C T U B K U N H G A C O F H O O
U F X I E Y O K I S J Y S N H V A E K E R P N L T
M F R T N P D J I V J F M A X V I Y N T G O S O I
F F R O H H A O R G A S M S T K C K Q M H M J L L
C Z Y G I L I Y M M W V Z P P Z C T L C L Z V F C
```

BASKETBALL
BLUEJEANS
BREAST
CLITORIS
DILDO
FEMALE
FINGER
HUG
KISS
LEATHER

LICK
MOTORCYCLE
NIPPLE
POTLUCK
SOFTBALL
TONGUE
VAGINA
WOMAN
BASTERBABY

BOOTS
BUTCH
COMINGOUT
EATOUT
FEMME
GAYBAR
JOCK
LAVENDER
LESBIAN
LOVER

MOUTH
ORGASM
SISTERHOOD
SUCK
TRUCK
VIBRATOR

#3 WORD SEARCH— CHANGES

Answers on page— 116

```
W R D Z Z W C Y F Y M W K P P A S I V P A I W E D
T F W W R P O S B T G M L X I E T C P Q G W H C I
Z E N K K E L R K F G X U A U C Y T F Y T T U T Z
V L X H E D L R N U B W P M I N W U N N J S N S C
J Y G N B D E S U R V I V O R C Y Z E G P I V I W
W M K T U J C N M J M B X G X S O M O O Z V X T D
E V Z O W F T W R Y A F Q N C U R S P B Q I V A S
N O I T A Z I N I M E F L G Z E O O O D Y T I R H
W W M H Y E V A I C N Q K K W W M B Y M K C K A Y
T X H U E K E F X O Z D C O O G U S S P O A F P Q
Y T I N U M M O C N S K P H L Q F J N D E H N E O
L C K A F M H Y F S U M N L A U X E S I B A Y S R
S T O N E W A L L C E U D A N Y O X V H I W J D T
A L E S B I A N S I P G J C D Q W V U R L Y D H M
R L A U X E S O M O H A T A I E S M A Y F G L P S
C G V Z T R M K D U T I T Y N O I T U L O V E R I
H N I E B M O K K S O J A R J L I R E V B N I V N
A I J L C Y A H H N V G G M I R A R F I S G O D I
I P Y Q Q T V R A E C T F D O A G C J N N G S F M
C P J V Y Z U L I S I A L H X S R W I H C E F T E
P A J T V I J D G S W X T I K F G C M D O J M B F
Q R I L N C U W G T A U C R I N S S H J A H K O Y
T N S B I N J J G M A Y W P K X N X U A Y R T Q I
U J F Z Z V G Q A B K F D K O Q W G F Z L O V J H
E K Z R E M O B H S P P F V X D P O Y G D I R X P
```

ACTIVIST
AUTHORITARIAN
COLLECTIVE
CONSCIOUSNESS
EMPOWERMENT
FEMINIZATION
GAY
HOMOSOCIAL
PATRIARCHAL

RAPPING
SEPARATIST
STONEWALL
UNITY
ARCHAIC
BISEXUAL
COMMUNITY
DYSFUNCTIONAL
FEMINISM

FRIEDAN
HOMOSEXUAL
LESBIAN
RADICAL
REVOLUTION
STEINEM
SURVIVOR

#4 WORD SEARCH—WOMEN

Answers on page—116

```
C A R O L G I L L I G A N H Y O W H L T H N T R B
M D X E L D R M F K C O L A F I S L F E D R E E B
A M B N J L E A I E T D R V L S A W A M K U L N W
R F A Y I F A F C R R R C L A C B T M A J B L G A
T A Z R J E X D A I U R A H A M H X T R M P I A L
I B P H I R T S O M E C A B E E Y E Y G E E M W I
N N H V C L Y S E O A A N R R K A U E A R H E Y C
A G O I A A Y N E T G E L B O N L E S R Y S T A E
H R J S M U N N H D R E I L D R V D S E L S A S B
E R I E M A O E M U U S N A E D M I O T S E K D T
S R E T A A R L A O H R L A M N A A F M T L C N O
A E O V A N I L E O N L T Q J Y R M E E R G A I K
M D L O A M B L P G I R V R D O G E N A E N G L L
O I O U M E A A L E N R O F E S A L A D E O N Y A
H R H C C R W E K I Y A U E Q G R I I P P R E C S
T Y P N Y Y E Y B E W H A E J B E A D A N A Y R I
O L P R H Z B L E R R S R Y D R T E N T O H A E V
L L A M J Z G A Y N O M I S A A S A O B S S N I A
R A S T I K Y U L T R W I R I M A R T E R N D P D
A S T Y N E D A Y L Y U N L C C N H N N E O L E E
M O T H E R G O O S E R O R L K G A I A T R A G T
M O T H E R T H E R E S A G E E E R H T N R C R T
B E T T Y F R I E D A N Z M I H R T E A I E E A B
R E K L A W E C I L A X B L F S C L S R W F Y M B
N O T N I L C E T A K N A M O W C I N O I B B V T
```

ALICEBTOKLAS
AMELIAEARHART
BETTEDAVIS
BIONICWOMAN
CAROLGILLIGAN
CRISWILLIAMSON
FERRARO
GERTRUDESTEIN
GRACIEALLEN
HEPBURN
SAPPHO
SEHINTON
SIGOURNEYWEAVER

JEANBAKERMILLER
KATECLINTON
LAURENBACALL
LUCYBALL
MARGARETSANGER
MARILYNMONROE
MARTINA
MAYAANGELOU
MERYLSTREEP
MOTHERTHERESA
RITAMAEBROWN
WILLACATHER
SALLYRIDE

SHARONGLESS
TYNEDALY
WINTERSON
ALICEWALKER
ANNEMURRAY
BETTYFRIEDAN
CAGNEYANDLACEY
CHER
DIANEFOSSEY
FERRON
GOD
HEATHERBISHOP
JANEGOODAL

KATEANDALLIE
KATEMILLET
LINDSAYWAGNER
MARGARETMEAD
MARGEPIERCY
MARLOTHOMAS
MAYSARTON
MARYTYLERMOORE
MOTHERGOOSE
PATBENETAR

#5 WORD SEARCH—SEX

Answers on page—116

```
N O I T C U D E S W T L E S B I A N M Y T H S J K
M Y T I D U N S H A R I N G O H F S Z P S R O G D
S A U T E R U S C O H P P A S U M X U E O Y D X X
M P S S H T A E D E L T T I L E T B I T O P M Y E
R A O T H J R A N I G A V X L N E K A F E U E T S
G S R R U G N I Y A L P E L O R C R S R L K N T P
R N E R N R I O A N S U S I T I B E F T Y L S E U
M E I X I O B H H H Y E T Y U I X U I S T A T R G
G S T K U A G A T H C A X Q V K M P S A I T R P N
Y N A A C A G R T D C I L I J E L F K D U W U G I
Q E I G E U L E A I N L B P S E S V I O C O A N D
C G S P R H S A R P O A S U O M R P N M S L T I N
I A H E Y O T B N V H N S R P E E S G A I L I T A
A S A S H T U E E A O Y G G H A H U N S M I O T T
T S V U T L O M L I T A N T E G T N I O O P N I S
R A I A O O A R T T S O A O M L O E N C R A M S T
U M N P Y K Y O E M T E M I S W M V I H P K I R O
C D G O I O L S S T L I N Y I A N F N I N I R U N
K T E N D E R N E S S T L E H K A O Y S A S R E G
D Z G E M S I D A B I R T L C I I S T M V S O Y U
R R O M A N C E V M E S O N O N B D X M E I R O E
I H T U O M J E A L O U S Y S G S N I N L N S V S
V U L V A T U C K I N G M L A D E U S F R G G L B
E R O L E S Y O B M O T F C M K L O Y P A R E H T
R L D F F O E D A R T S O B S E L M S S E N T E W
```

INTIMACY
JOYOFSEX
LEATHER
LESBIANMOTHERS
LESBOS
LITTLETHEATER
LOVE
LUBRICATION
MASOCHISM
MASTURBATION
MENSTRUATION
MOUNDSOFVENUS
MULTIPLEORGASMS
ROLES

NOSE
ORGASM
PERFUMES
PLAY
PROMISCUITY
PUBICHAIR
ROLEPLAYING
ROMANCE
SAPPHO
SEXISM
SHARING
SITTINGPRETTY
SKIN

STANDINGUPSEX
SUCKING
THERAPY
TONGUES
TRADEOFF
TRUCKDRIVER
UTERUS
VIBRATORS
VULVA
WETNESS
JEALOUSY
KISSING
LEGSANDTHIGHS
LESBIANMYTHS

LITTLEDEATH
LOTIONS
LOVEMAKING
MARRIAGE
MASSAGE
MENOPAUSE
MIRRORS
MOUTH
NAVEL
NUDITY
OUT
PILLOWTALK
PORNOGRAPHY
PUBERTY
QUICKIES

SADOMASOCHISM
SEDUCTION
SEXUALANATOMY
SHAVING
SIXTYNINING
SMELLS
STEREOTYPING
TENDERNESS
TOMBOYS
TOYS
TRIBADISM
TUCKING
VAGINA
VOYEURS
WAKING

29

#6 WORD SEARCH—MORE SEX

Answers on page—116

```
B T V L U F F E M I N I S M B L O W I N G S M W I
U N I A D I L D O S F G Y C N E U Q E R F W R G V
T U F S D O V G E O E A F G S G N I T I B I G A P
C C E U M C T H R N L I F C F T C E L I B A C Y B
H W A O X K S E T P N R W P P X H F I D E L I T Y
I O T R I U P L S G I F U C K I N G Y S A T N A F
F F H A R L E I E G E D I S C R I M I N A T I O N
F L E C A N D R I R N M D R A G S N X R C R W A H
O A R Y E O S D Z I Q E E B I S E X U A L I T Y P
G G S S E N I L N A E L C R R C E F G O O I S C N
N E S J T T L I T H S S V A C M L M B S S T V O N
I L P R Y S E K Y D N C E F M A S O E U E Q I I E
H L D E B N I T S A F K A E R B L N T R T S L N C
S A U R W H C H G B D S F I U E O E E H S D I X N
I T N P E L O E O R A G T T S Z G C D E E L S E E
N I Q D I D N L E R T C T I S I T A R E P S T G N
I O D T I I L S D U N O K U P O D P D I M E N I I
F N L A T C S O O I C I O R M M E O C N O E A C T
C I G A N E A G G K N N N Y U D R S R T O D R E S
T H L N D C N P S N E G B E R B I A G H V B O C B
S I E S I I I H P G I O O U S D S I Y Q P W D U A
A D E E M G R N O E O W G U N S B H S U B A O B S
E X E O K F A R G T D S O G T A L C O H O L E E U
V T C B E S E L S B A T H R O O M S D N A H D S N
Z C L I T O R I S E Y E S H G E R O T I C I S M A
```

ABSTINENCE	CLEANLINESS	FANTASY	BACKRUBS	DISCIPLINE
ALCOHOL	CLITORIS	FEMINISM	BATHROOMS	DISPLAY
APHRODISIACS	CLOTHES	FIDELITY	BIGTOE	DRESSEDSEX
AROUSAL	CREMEDELACREME	FINISHINGOFF	BITING	DYKES
BARS	CUNT	FOREPLAY	BONDAGE	EYES
BEDS	DEODORANTS	FRIGIDITY	BUTCH	FEATHERS
BISEXUALITY	DILDOS	GENITALIA	CELIBACY	FEMME
BLOWING	DISCRIMINATION	GROWINGOLDER	COMINGOUT	FINGERS
BOOTS	DRAG	HANDICAPPED	CIVILRIGHTS	FLAGELLATION
BUSH	DRUGS	HOLDINGOUT	CLITLIT	FREQUENCY
BUTTOCKS	EARS	HYSTERECTOMY	CLOSETS	FUCKING
CHEEKS	EROTICISM	AGING	CRUSHES	GENTLENESS
HORNINESS	BREAKFASTINBED	ANUS	DANCING	HAIR
ICECUBES	EROGENOUSZONES	ARMPITS	DEPRESSION	HANDS

CRYSTAL CLEAR

Fill in the boxes below to complete the correct five-letter horizontal words so that each rectangle will spell the name of a crystal or gemstone. An example is given to get you started. Answers given on page—117

EXAMPLE:
D R **O** N E
A P **P** L Y
S T **A** R T
A L **L** O T

1. (RUBY)
DA **R** TS
PR **U** NE
GA **B** LE
KA **Y** AK

2. (AMBER)
DR **A** NK
CA **M** EL
TA **B** LE
BE **E** TS
AC **R** ID

3. (FOSSIL)
AW **F** UL
BO **O** TS
ME **S** SY
RE **S** ET
CO **I** LS
TI **L** ES

4. (SUNSTONE)
BA **S** TE
GR **U** NT
FI **N** AL
AS **S** ET
TI **T** LE
BR **O** OM
FU **N** NY
RE **E** DS

5. (PERIDOT)
LA **P** EL
ST **E** AL
MO **R** ON
NA **I** LS
RA **D** AR
WR **O** TE
MI **T** ES

6. (CARNELIAN)
UN **C** LE
BR **A** VE
CA **R** AT
RU **N** NY
CR **E** ST
CO **L** OR
DR **I** NK
PR **A** WN
IN **N** ER

MORE CRYSTAL CLEAR

1.

P E		C H
W O		A N
S M		L L
R A		E D
S T		K E
S A		D S
B R		C K
B A		I K
S T		R N

2.

S A		E R
W A		K S
F A		L T
S H		R T
M A		C H
S T		N T
A C		O R
A M		N D

3.

P I		O T
C R		N K
H A		P Y
H E		S T
M I		T Y
S A		T Y
L E		V E
M A		E S
P R		N E
S A		A D
P R		M E

4.

F O		T S
O T		E R
L O		N Y
L O		E S
W R		T E
R A		K S
W A		M S
S W		O N
S I		S Y
W R		S T
A F		E R
S M		L L

5.

B A		E S
P E		R S
A P		L E
D E		O T
A S		E N
B R		N E
P O		C H
T R		A T

6.

B O		C H
S M		K E
T R		S T
C O		N S
T I		E D
B E		D S
M O		E S
T W		C E
D E		T S
W E		K S

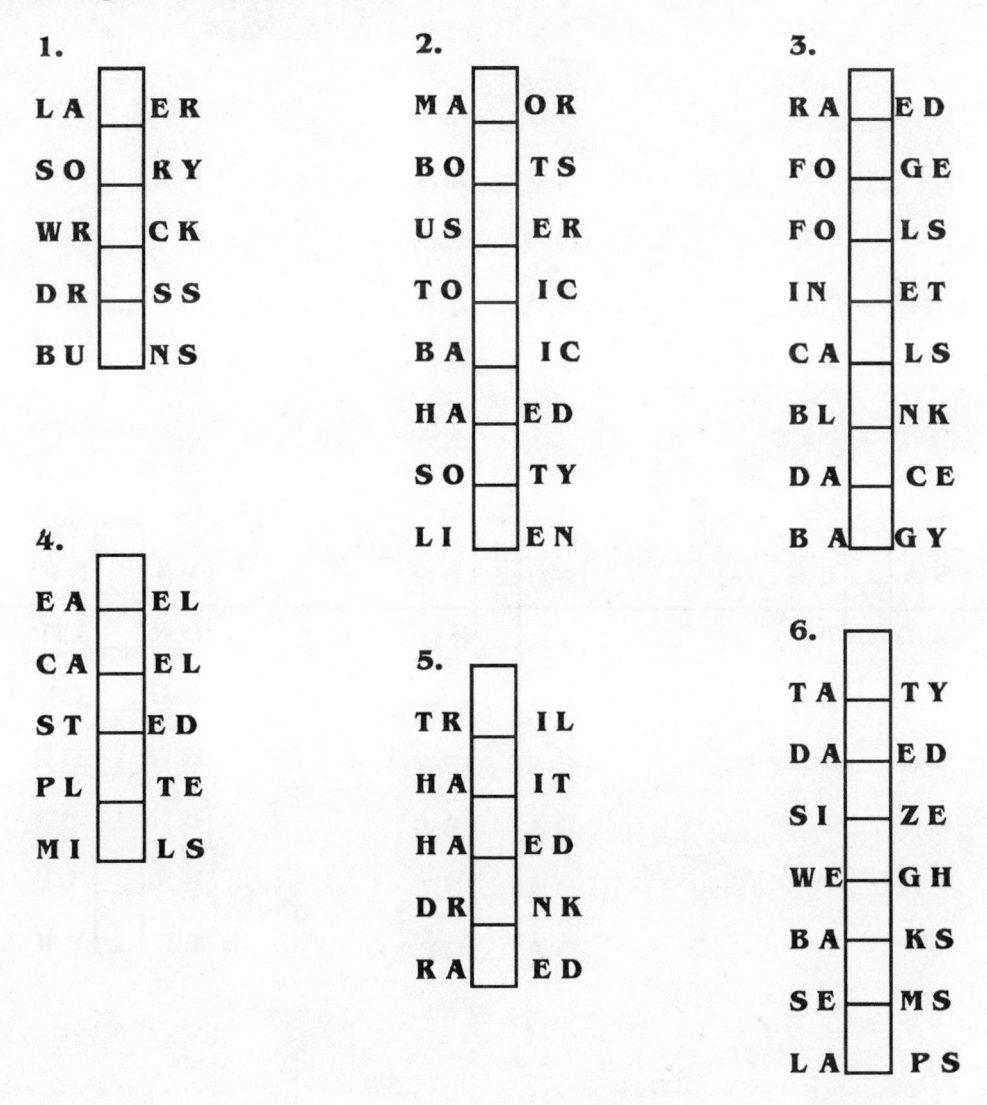

WOMEN OF THE SEVENTIES

Fill in the boxes below to complete the correct five-letter horizontal words so that each rectangle will spell the name of an American woman significant to the feminist movement of the 1970 s.
Answers given on page—117

1.

LA _ ER
SO _ RY
WR _ CK
DR _ SS
BU _ NS

2.

MA _ OR
BO _ TS
US _ ER
TO _ IC
BA _ IC
HA _ ED
SO _ TY
LI _ EN

3.

RA _ ED
FO _ GE
FO _ LS
IN _ ET
CA _ LS
BL _ NK
DA _ CE
BA _ GY

4.

EA _ EL
CA _ EL
ST _ ED
PL _ TE
MI _ LS

5.

TR _ IL
HA _ IT
HA _ ED
DR _ NK
RA _ ED

6.

TA _ TY
DA _ ED
SI _ ZE
WE _ GH
BA _ KS
SE _ MS
LA _ PS

33

MORE WOMEN OF THE SEVENTIES

Fill in the boxes below to complete the correct five-letter horizontal words so that each rectangle will spell the name of an American woman significant to the feminist movement of the 1970 s.
Answers given on page—117

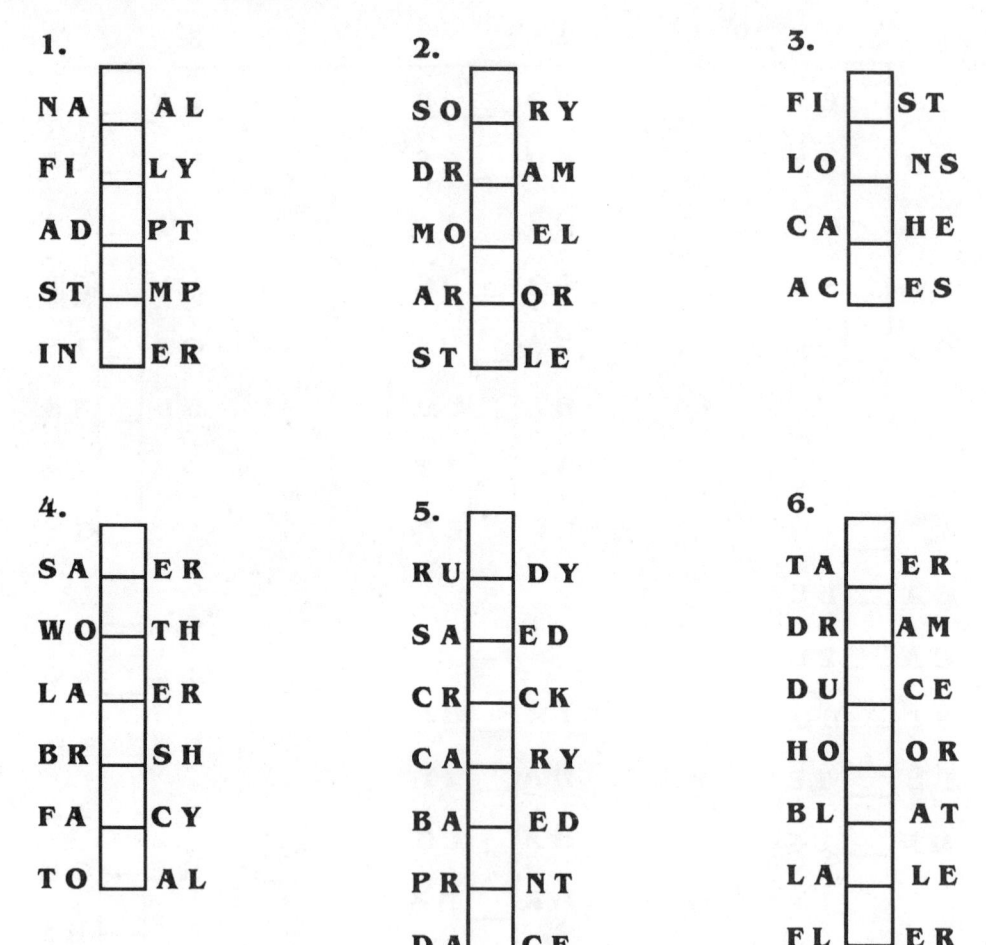

1.
NA _ AL
FI _ LY
AD _ PT
ST _ MP
IN _ ER

2.
SO _ RY
DR _ AM
MO _ EL
AR _ OR
ST _ LE

3.
FI _ ST
LO _ NS
CA _ HE
AC _ ES

4.
SA _ ER
WO _ TH
LA _ ER
BR _ SH
FA _ CY
TO _ AL

5.
RU _ DY
SA _ ED
CR _ CK
CA _ RY
BA _ ED
PR _ NT
DA _ CE

6.
TA _ ER
DR _ AM
DU _ CE
HO _ OR
BL _ AT
LA _ LE
FL _ ER

34

SISTER COLLEGES

Fill in the boxes below to complete the correct five-letter horizontal words so that each rectangle will spell the name of one of the sister colleges. Answers given on page—117

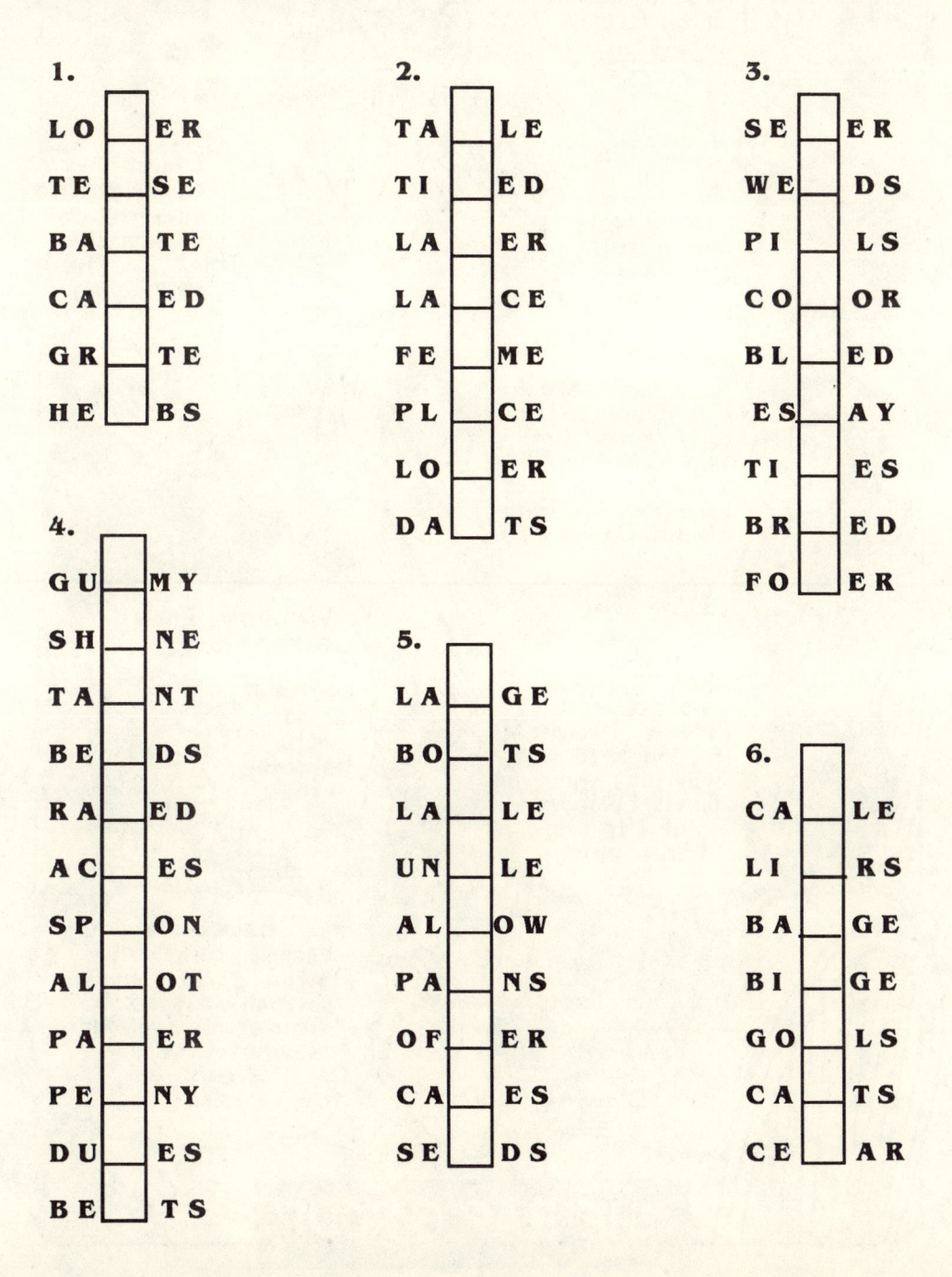

1.

L O	_	E R
T E	_	S E
B A	_	T E
C A	_	E D
G R	_	T E
H E	_	B S

2.

T A	_	L E
T I	_	E D
L A	_	E R
L A	_	C E
F E	_	M E
P L	_	C E
L O	_	E R
D A	_	T S

3.

S E	_	E R
W E	_	D S
P I	_	L S
C O	_	O R
B L	_	E D
E S	_	A Y
T I	_	E S
B R	_	E D
F O	_	E R

4.

G U	_	M Y
S H	_	N E
T A	_	N T
B E	_	D S
R A	_	E D
A C	_	E S
S P	_	O N
A L	_	O T
P A	_	E R
P E	_	N Y
D U	_	E S
B E	_	T S

5.

L A	_	G E
B O	_	T S
L A	_	L E
U N	_	L E
A L	_	O W
P A	_	N S
O F	_	E R
C A	_	E S
S E	_	D S

6.

C A	_	L E
L I	_	R S
B A	_	G E
B I	_	G E
G O	_	L S
C A	_	T S
C E	_	A R

35

THE RAP GROUP

Facilitator: ...So the **topic** for tonight's discussion is "Being Lesbian in a Clitorially Naive, Ageist, Sexist Racist and Weight-Conscious Society". Let's go around the room and share our thoughts, starting on my **left**!

Free associator: I'm really, really **happy** to be here. I'm not sure what I'd like to say, so I think I'll just **free associate** for a while...

Horny one (thinking): I'm going to be right out the **door** in two minutes... why did I have to be **horny** on a Tuesday night?

Uncertain one: But how do **I** really feel? Hmmm... I just don't **know**!

Article rememberer (thinking): I must have read an **article** somewhere on this subject... **Think**! **Think**!

Off-topic one: O I don't **care** if it relates to the topic or **not**! I'm talking about the "Walk to Prevent Irradiated Food from being Force Fed to Dolphins"!

Anxious one: I wonder what I'll **say**... I wonder what I **think**... I wonder if I can **pass** when it's my turn... I wonder if I'll **throw up**!

Newcomer (thinking): Well, **now** I know a **rap** group has **nothing** to do with hammer-ing!

Jock: I **hate** being between basketball, rugby, soccer, and softball seasons. As soon as it's daylight savings time, I'm **out** of here!

TO A TEE

Each of the words and phrases below applies to softball and contains the letter T. You're batting a thousand if you can guess them all. Answers given on page—115

1. "_ _ _ _ _ _ _ T!"
2. _ _ _ _ T _ _ _ _
3. _ _ T
4. _ T _ _ _
5. "_ _ T T _ _ _ _."
6. _ T _ _ _ _
7. _ _ T T _ _ _ _ _ _ _ _
8. _ _ _ _ T _ _ _ _
9. _ _ _ T _ _ _ _ _ _
10. _ _ _ _ T
11. _ _ _ _ _ _ _ _ T _
12. T _ _ _ _ _ _
13. _ _ _ _ _ T _
14. _ _ _ T _ _ _ _ _ _
15. _ _ T _ _ _ _
16. _ _ T _ _ _ _ _
17. _ _ T
18. T _ _ _
19. _ _ T _ _ _ _ _ _
20. _ _ _ _ _ T _ T _ _
21. _ _ T _ _ _ _

ACROSTICS

#1 HEROINES

Fill in the names of these famous women in the spaces provided.

```
_ _ _ _ H _ _ _
_ _ _ _ _ E _ _ _ _ _
_ _ R _ _ _ _
_ _ _ _ _ O _ _ _ _
_ _ _ _ I _
_ _ _ _ _ _ _ N _ _
_ _ E _ _ _ _
_ _ S _ _ _
```

1) A journalist, she established the first women-owned brokerage firm on Wall Street and ran for President of the United States in 1872.

2) She went to the Crimea in 1854 to organize health care for the British troops, who were dying as much from disease and unsanitary conditions as from wounds.

3) First name of a woman writer who marched for civil rights in Selma, and later was in the forefront of the lesbian rights movement. Her first book, *Prison Notes,* was written in jail.

4) In 1429 she led 10,000 troops to battle against the English to drive them out of France.

5) First name of the woman pilot who broke records for speed, distance, altitude, and solo flights from 1928 to 1937.

6) A powerful speaker on the issues of women's rights, racism, and non-violence. After the Emancipation Proclamation, she devoted her time to helping freed men and women to make it on their own.

7) One of the founders of the third wave of feminism, she later founded a major women's magazine.

8) She devoted her life, and her death, to saving the mountain gorillas.

Answers to Acrostics found on page 115

ACROSTICS

#2 HERSTORY

```
    _ _ _ _ _ H _
_ _ _ _ _ _ _ _ E _
      _ _ _ R _ _ _
    _ _ _ _ S _ _ _ _
      _ _ T _ _ _ _
      _ O _ _ _ _ _ _ _
    _ _ _ _ _ R _ _
      _ _ _ _ _ Y
```

1) The woman who made lesbianism famous

2) A courageous Indian guide and explorer who, carrying her infant son on her back, led Lewis and Clark through 5000 miles of wilderness on a journey that earned them great fame.

3) An American expatriate whose salons in Paris were attended by all the exciting and interesting lesbians of her day. (Clue- It's not Gertrude Stein.)

4) She became queen of Sweden in 1644 at the age of 18. She was known for her habit of dressing in men's clothing and for not hiding her affection for other women.

5) Born in 1875, black, and one of 17 children, she managed to get an education and eventually to establish a school for Negro girls. In 1933 President Roosevelt made her Director of the Division of Negro Affairs.

6) A queen of Britain who lead an attack against the Romans when they tried to confiscate her lands. She and her daughters led the defense from chariots, but were eventually beaten.

7) Uninterested in "womanly pursuits," she dressed in men's clothing and enlisted in the army. She fought courageously in the Revolutionary War for 3 years before coming down with cholera and having her true gender discovered. (first name)

8) Along with Mary Read, she is famous for being a woman pirate.

Much of this information was taken from *Generations of Denial* by Kathryn Taylor, published by Times Change Press in 1971.
Answers to Acrostics found on page 115

ACROSTICS

3 WOMEN'S SPORTS

```
            W _ _ _ _              S _ _
            _ O _ _ _ _            P _ _ _ _ _ _
    _ _ _ _ _ _ _ M _ _            _ O _ _
    _ _ _ _ _ E _ _ _ _            _ _ R _ _ _ _ _
            N _ _ _                _ _ _ _ _ T
        _ _ _ _ S                  S _ _ _ _
```

1) She overcame polio to eventually become one of the world's fastest runners. (first name)

2) She was the fastest and most stylish runner in the 1988 Olympics.

3) She is known for her excellence in basketball and her "friendship" with Martina.

4) A founder of the women's sports foundation, she put women's tennis on the map.

5) A long distance swimmer

6) A 16-year-old swimmer who broke many records at the 1988 Olympics

7) An all-round athlete, she played golf and competed in the Olympics in track and field, winning a gold medal in 1932.

8) She portrayed one of the athletes (the one we all fell madly in love with) in the movie *Personal Best*. (first name)

9) One of the fastest pitchers in the history of softball

10) The tennis champion who proved that women could play as aggressive a game as men

11) The first woman to win the Olympic marathon

12) An Olympic champion figure skater who later turned her talent to movies. (first name)

Answers to Acrostics found on page 115

ACROSTICS

4 PIONEERS

```
    _ _ P _ _ _ _
  _ _ _ I _ - _ _ _ _
    _ _ O _ _ _ _
    _ _ N _ _
  _ _ _ _ E _
    _ E _ _ _
    _ _ R _ _
    S _ _ _ _
```

1) Greek woman mathematician murdered in Alexandria

2) A French woman who disguised herself as a beggar and walked to Lhasa, the capital of Tibet. She later published a scholarly work entitled *Magic and Mystery in Tibet*.

3) A pioneer in the field of primate research, she has spent over 20 years in Africa studying chimpanzees.

4) The first name of a straight-shooting, hard-riding western woman who became a legend by touring the country as part of Buffalo Bill's Wild West show.

5) A Lesbian novelist who wrote about women pioneers and who became one of America's greatest writers. Her novel *My Antonia* has been required reading for most teenagers.

6) First name of a woman who flew as a bush pilot in Africa in the 1930's and in 1936 was the first person to fly the Atlantic solo the hard way - east to west.

7) A woman whose name has become synonomous with the discovery of radiation.

8) The first American woman to fly into space (first name)

Answers to Acrostics found on page 115

ACROSTICS

#5 MATRIARCHY (reference—*Mothers and Amazons* by Helen Diner, Anchor Press, 1973)

```
      _ _ M _ _ _ _
          A _ _ _ _ _ _ _
      _ _ T _ _ _ _
_ _ _ _ _ _ _ R _
          _ I _ _ _
          _ A _ _
      _ _ _ R _ _
    _ _ _ _ _ C _
          H _ _ _ _
          _ Y _ _
```

1) The Mother Goddess of the Greeks—mother of Persephone

2) Women warriors who are reputed to have conquered much of the middle east at one time

3) Goddess of the warrior women of Ephesus

4) A queen of North Africa

5) A country in Asia where polyandry is common

6) The Indian great mother goddess of birth, life, and death who wears a necklace of sculls

7) The weapon found in the Minoan mazes

8) An Iroquois Indian matriarchal tribe as well as home town of American feminism

9) The totem animal of the Amazons

10) A matriarchal tribe of Borneo

Answers to Acrostics found on page 115

CLASSIC VOWELS

In this puzzle only the vowels A, E, I, O, and U are given. Column 1 contains the names of some classic lesbian-themed book titles; column 2 lists their authors. Fill in the missing letters, then match the authors to their books. Answers given on page—115

Column 1: Books

_ e e _ o _ _ i _ _ e _

_ u _ _ _ _ u i _ _ u _ _ _ _ e

_ _ e _ a _ i e _

_ a _ i e _ _ e a _ _ _ a _ a _

_ e _ _ o _ _ o _ e _ i _ e _ _

_ i _ a

_ _ o i _ e _

_ e _ e _ _ o _ _ _ e

_ e a _ _

Column 2: Authors

_ a _ e _ u _ e

i _ a _ e _ _ i _ _ e _

_ a _ e _ i _ _ e _

_ i _ a _ a e _ _ o _ _ _

_ a _ _ _ _ _ _ e _ a _ _

a _ _ _ a _ _ o _

_ a _ _ _ _ o _ e _

_ o _ i _ _ _ u _ _ a _ _

43

JUMBLES

Unscramble these Jumbles, one letter to a square, to form ordinary words. Answers on page— 115

#1   What the woman picked up from her hand-held lover

TEIOLT

IOLIVN

OBRKSO

RDGNIAG

Now arrange the circled letters to form the surprise answer suggested by the above cartoon.

#2   How she introduced her former lover's former lover to her current lover.

LDEICYTXE

AIMED

MPXAESLE

TYEJT

"HONEY,

44

JUMBLES

#3 Where the uptight lesbian keeps her hang-ups.

ECLUN

STOIM

YRSIPC

HCAET

#4 What the confused lesbian, upon reading the personals for the first time, thought LF stood for.

IILBATY

GIRFAEL

UMELTSAE

BLUSUEN

JUMBLES

#5 A lesbian quickie.

VAREB

MODEN

DRUNE

FATOL

#6 What the admiring woman called the strong body builder's chest appendages.

PRIGE

SWETOR

TTTHOREL

GTINGUS

JUMBLES

#7

The advice given when you want to break celibacy.

RJIUES

ABBY

AYNSER

SUTERREA

" ▢▢▢▢▢ ▢▢▢ ▢▢▢▢ "

#8

Three popular lesbian volleyball terms.

BEYAM

MPRAS

KAACBEHC

NUDET

▢▢▢▢▢ , ▢▢▢▢ , ▢▢▢▢

47

#1 NUMBERLESS— MEETINGPLACES

From the list below select the words that fit in the numberless puzzle.
Answers on page— 118

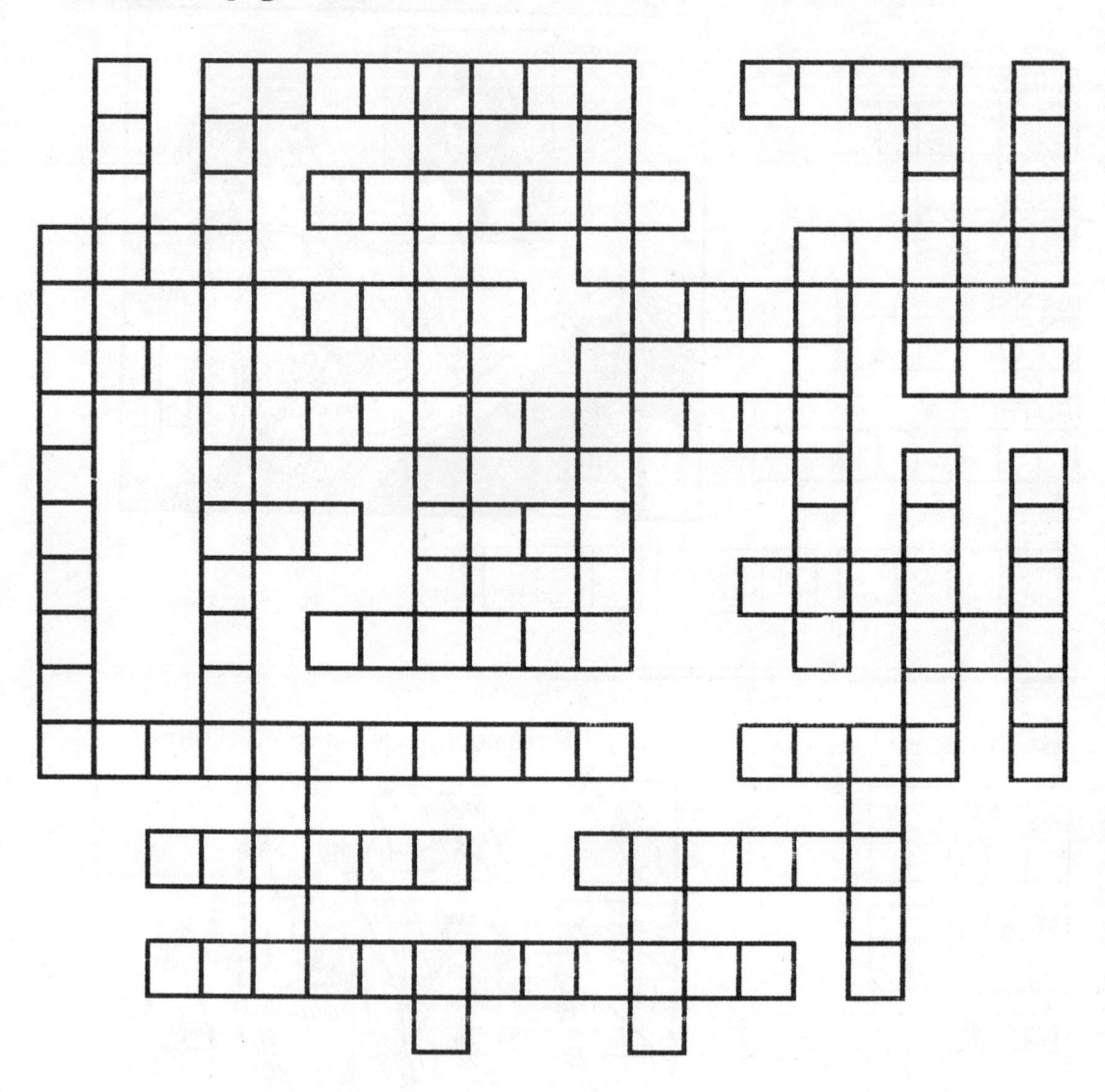

AA
BARS
BARN
BUSES
CAFE
CAR
CHURCH
COFFEEHOUSES
CONCERT
CRUISE
CONFERENCES
DANCES
DISCOS
FIRE
FRIENDSRUG
GUESTHOUSES
HOTELS
INNS
JOBS
LAKE
LESBIANGROUP
NAPLES
NAVY
NOW
PARTY
PARK
PERSONAL
POOL
SEA
SPORTS
STORES
TAXI
TOURS
WOMENSCENTERS
WORKCAMP

2 NUMBERLESS— F WORDS

**From the list below select the words that fit in the numberless puzzle.
Answers on page— 118**

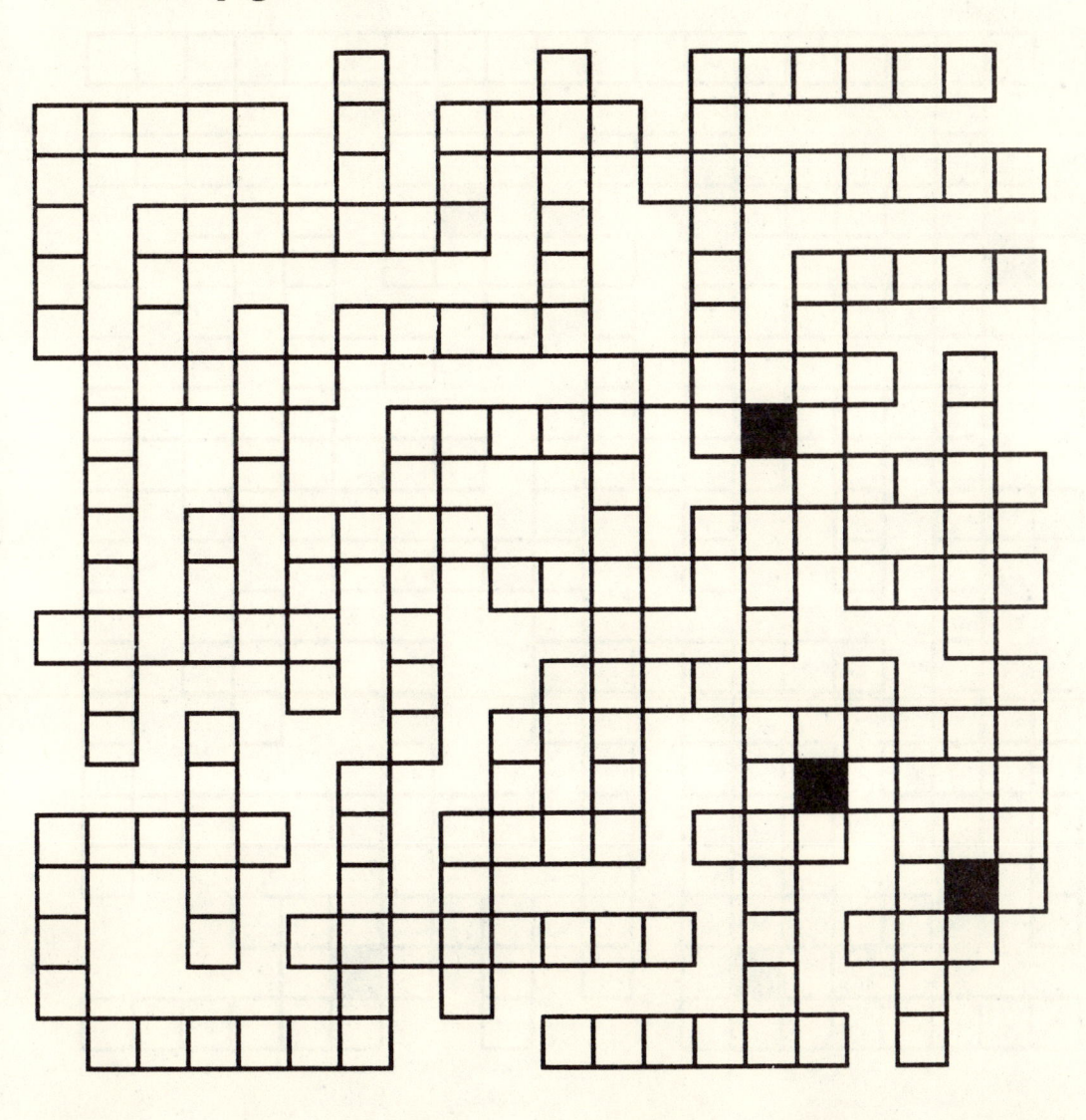

FACED	FEEL	FIG	FLINCH	FREAK	FUCK
FAINT	FEMME	FILE	FLOW	FREE	FUDGE
FANTASY	FENCE	FINGER	FLUFF	FRENCH	FUMBLE
FAN	FEVERISH	FIRM	FLY	FRIG	FUN
FANNY	FIB	FIST	FONDLE	FRILL	FUR
FANG	FICKLE	FITS	FOREPLAY	FRIGGA	FUSIONS
FAR	FIDDLE	FLAUNT	FORGO	FRICTION	
FAST	FIE	FLAGELLATE	FRENETIC	FROLIC	
FEAR	FIERCE	FLEA	FRANTIC	FRY	

3 NUMBERLESS—POLITICS

From the list below select the words that fit in the numberless puzzle.
Answers on page— 118

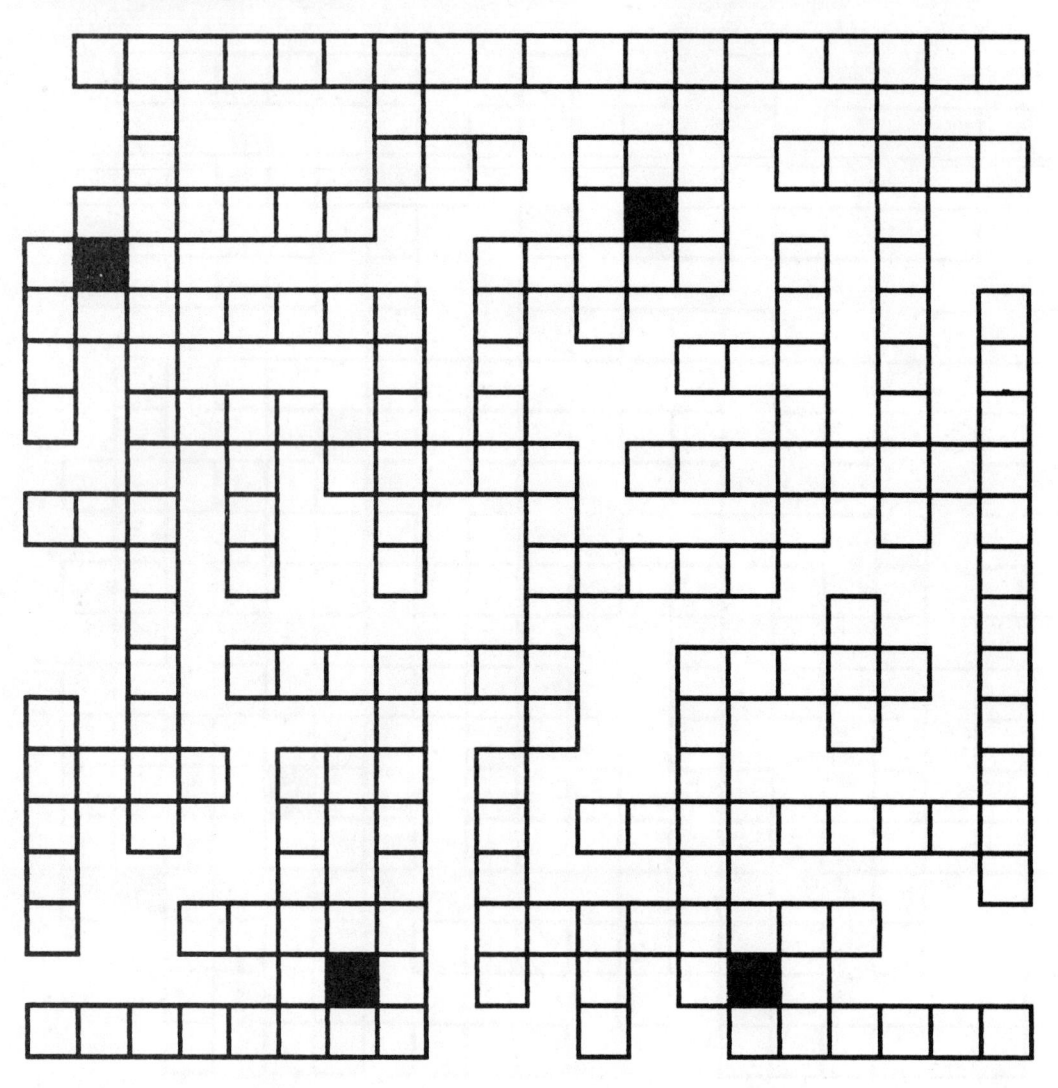

ABORTION	CHICANA	ELEANOR ROOSEVELT	MARCH	SEXISM
ABZUG	CHOICE	GAY MARRIAGES	MEN	TAX
ABUSE	CLASSISM	GUN	NATION	TIMES
ANTIWAR	CON	HOMELESS	NOW	TRUTH
BILL	CONGRESS	HOMOPHOBIA	PRIDE	TUBMAN
BLACK	EMMA	LAWS	PRO	USA
BOMBS	ERA	LESBIANANDGAYRIGHTS	RACISM	WAR
CAMPAIGN	ENABLE	LIES	RIGHT	YEARS
		PRIVILEGE	RULE	

4 NUMBERLESS— HOTSPOTS

**From the list below select the words that fit in the numberless puzzle.
Answers on page—118**

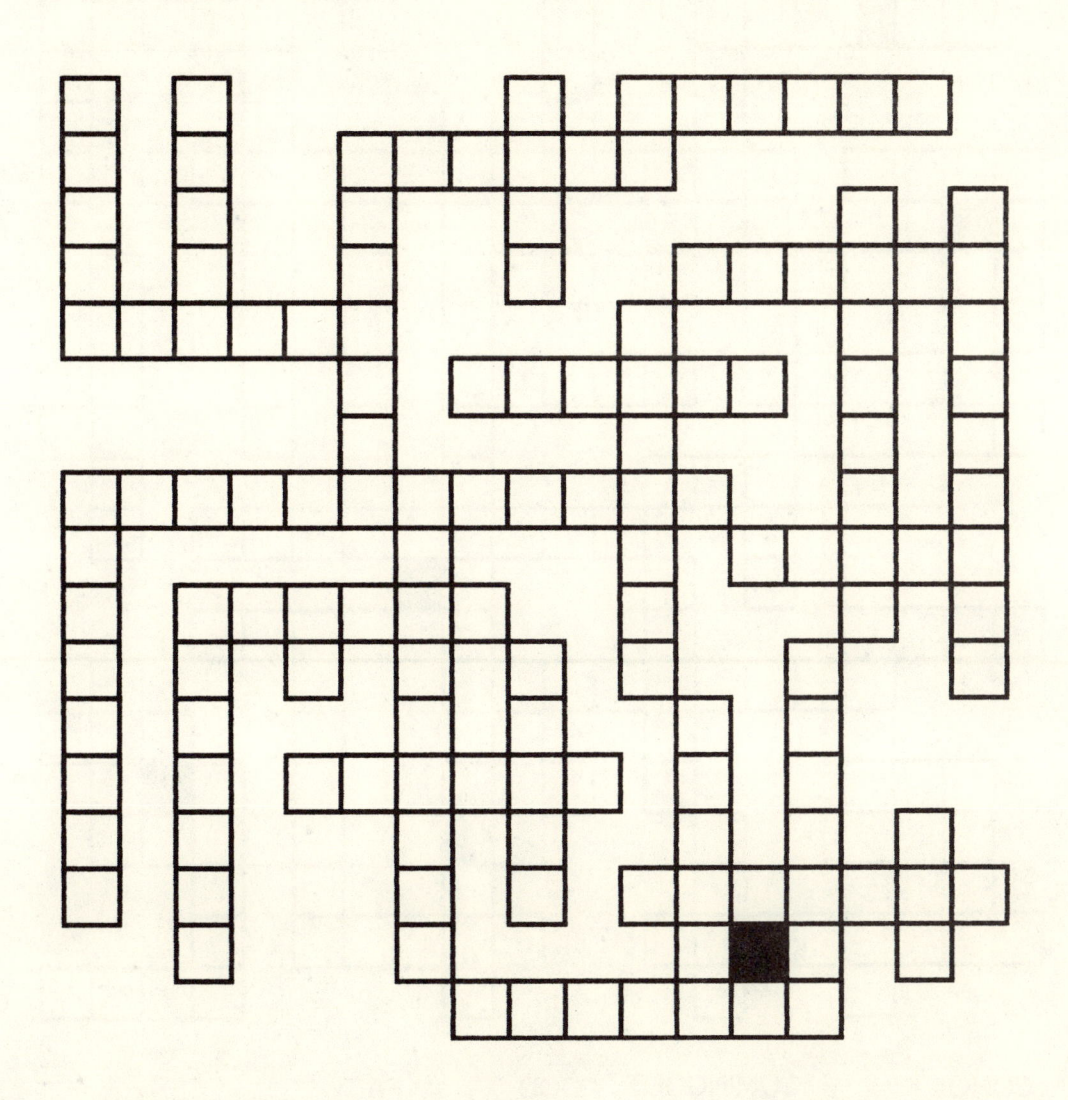

ARUBA	EUGENE	PHOENIX
AUSTIN	FARGO	PORTLAND
BALTIMORE	HARTFORD	PROVINCETOWN
BOSTON	KEYWEST	RENO
CANADA	LA	RIO
CLEVELAND	LONDON	ST CROIX
DALLAS	NY	ST LOUIS
DENVER	NYACK	TOPEKA
DETROIT	PARIS	TRENTON

5 NUMBERLESS— COUNSELING

From the list below select the words that fit in the numberless puzzle.
Answers on page— 118

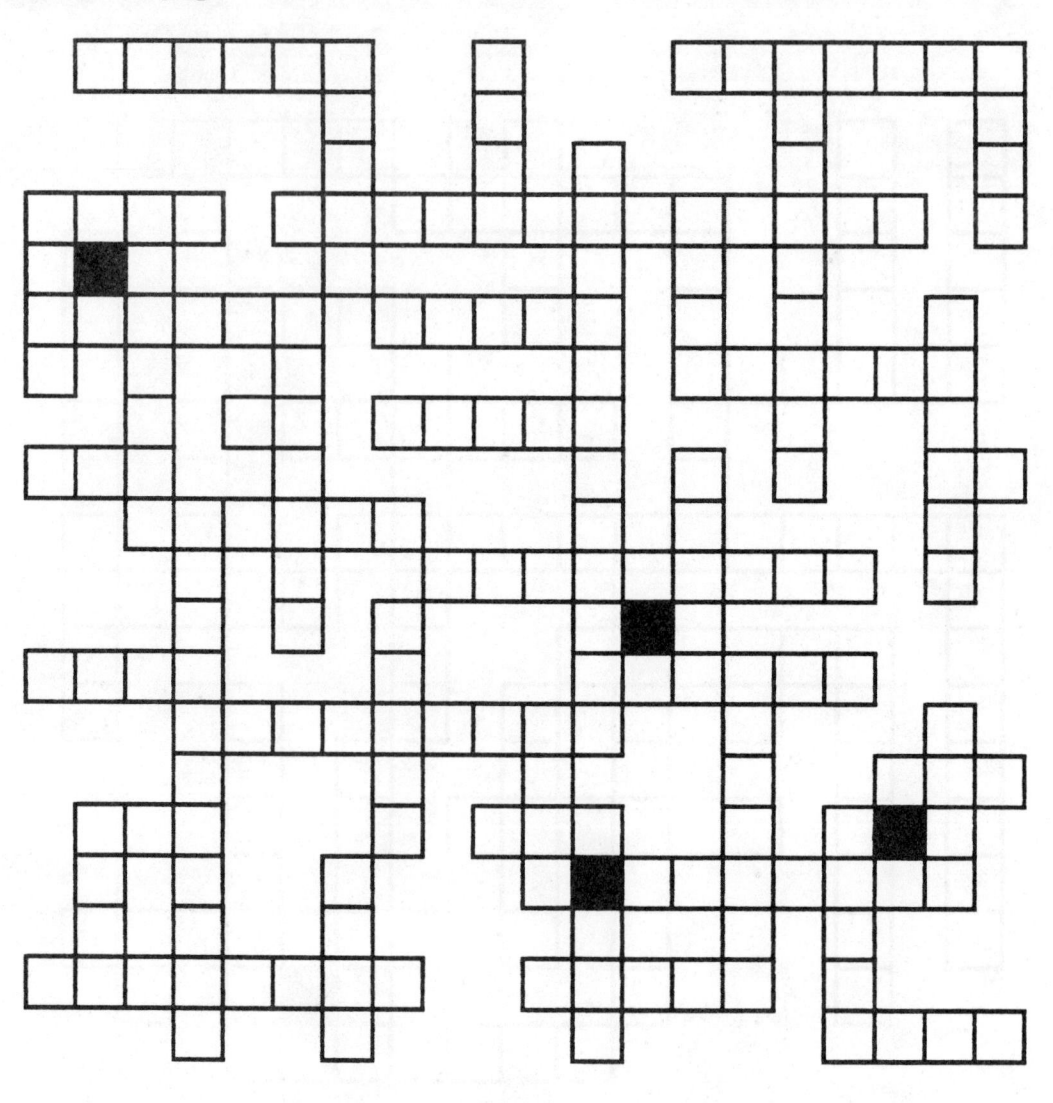

ALCOHOL	COMINGOUT	FOOD	PAST	SEX
ANGER	CONTROL	GAY	PHOBIA	SHAME
ANXIETY	DRUGS	GRIEFWORK	POWER	SING
CAREER	ENDINGS	GROWTH	PRIDE	STRESS
CHANGE	EX	IDENTITY	RACE	TEAR
CHOICES	FAT	LOVE	RAPE	TRAUMA
CODEPENDENCY	FATE	MEN	SANE	ABUSE
RELATIONSHIPS	FEARS	NO	SEXUALITY	AGE
TRANSITIONS	FEEL	PAIN		

52

6 NUMBERLESS— WRITERS

From the list below select the words that fit in the numberless puzzle.
Answers on page—118

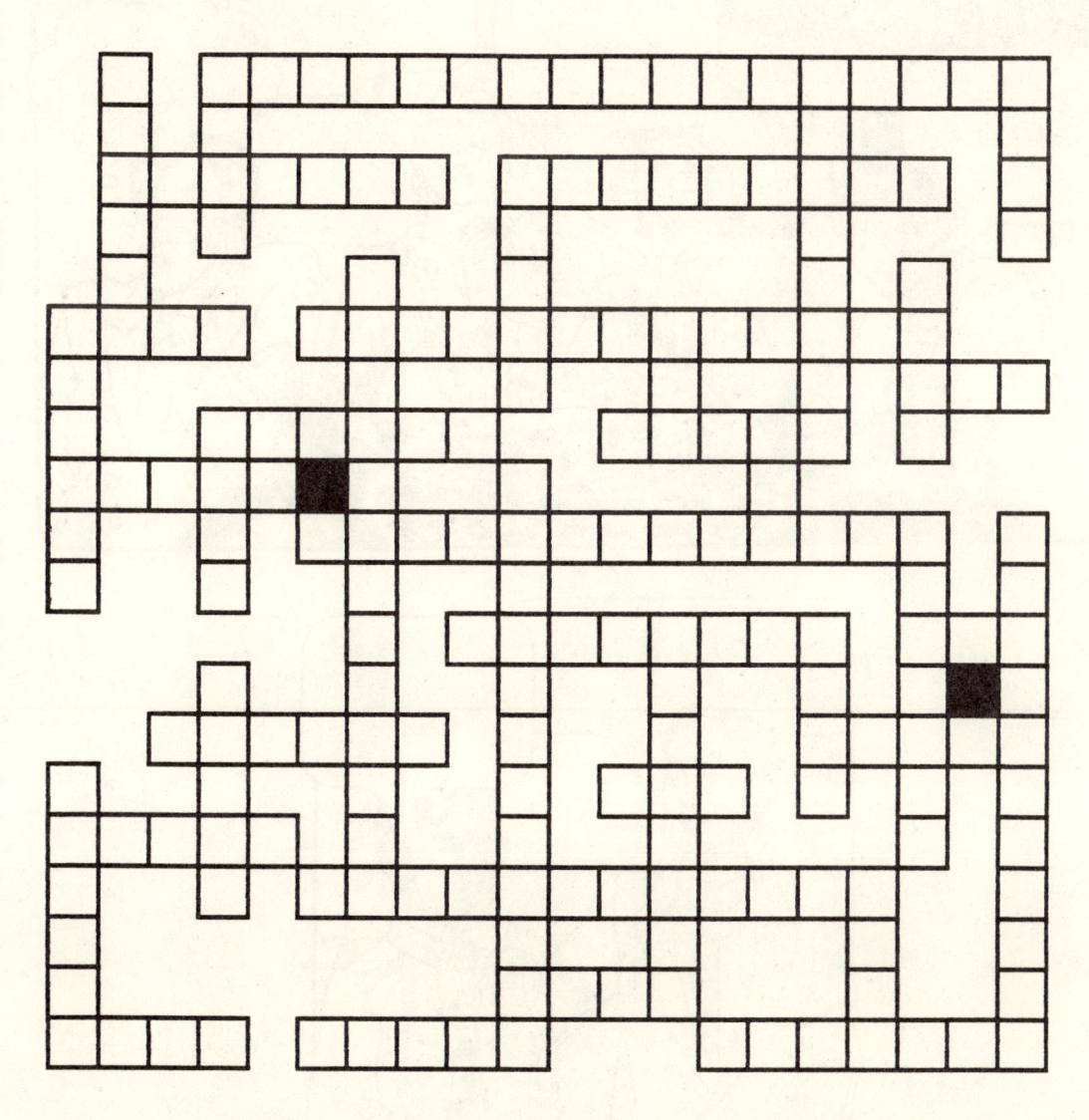

ACT	EDITOR	MAC	PRONOUN	VERB
BARNES	EPIGRAMS	NAIAD	RADCLYFFE HALL	ROLE
BOOK	EROTICISM	NOUN	RENEE VIVIAN	SAPPHO
COLON	FANTASY	NUN	RITA MAE BROWN	WHO
COMMA	FUN	PAGE	ROMANCED	WORD
DRAMA	HD	PHRASES	DYKE REACTION	
EARLY	JANERULE	PHRASE	NATALIE BARNEY	
EDIT	KNOWS	PLAY	VITA SACKVILLE WEST	
IMAGE	POETRY	TYPE	VIRGINIA WOOLF	

More Fill In The Bubbles

LET'S SPLIT A PIZZA

54

More Fill In The Bubbles

#1 CROSSWORD—AND ROMANCE

Answers on page— 117

#1 CROSSWORD—AND ROMANCE

ACROSS
2. our shape and the way we play the game
7. the sound of kissing
12. Freud's unconscious source of sex
14. the culmination of foreplay
15. ____ and games
16. where it often happens
18. motion of the tide
19. acronym for romantic natural art
20. a result of feeling turned on
21. what we often do after
23. everything else we haven't mentioned
25. a good come on
29. invasive sex toy— 2 words
31. ___ ...let's do it
32. another kind of curve
33. a very sexy fruit
34. 2 words- having fun together
36. not just referring to the weather
38. Earth goddess
40. trying it out
42. to make it even more fun
44. makes the deity of love happy
45. dilates when she is interested
46. a country word for breasts
48. what she does with food too
50. sexual ____, how we perform
52. rest
53. what we all dread for our relationships
55. our precious fluids
59. a donkey too
62. take a dainty drink
63. the *G* word
65. 2 words— you probably don't need one even if it's your first time
66. a turn on when nibbled
68. some people think he's cute
69. use the tongue
70. what we do to our lover and our cats
71. what we try to do to each other

DOWN
1. an abbreviation for our freedom
3. not a turn off
4. our very own mountain
5. colloquial for good
6. some people disapprove
7. other lips
8. it may not be love, but it can be fun
9. tongue to tongue
10. genital name (from the great goddess Kundi)
11. to have a talent
13. it's on spring grass as well
17. want, with passion
22. 3 words— our flavors
24. She called yesterday
26. what to do with those wild oats
27. used for hair and other body parts
28. ____ it with flowers
30. 2 words —lesbians don't have to read a book to figure out where one is
35. the _____ of her company
37. all the better to lick you with, my dear
39. 2 words—a sexual power center
41. some lesbians do it this way
43. a non-sexual therapy
47. can do
49. getting close
50. 2 words — babies love it too
51. to pull
54. what we don't want to hear from our lovers
56. matriarchal state of India
57. a woman's name
58. holds, moistens, or maneuvers in the mouth
60. What we seldom want to do
61. women together
63. a word for having
64. our latest lover
65. everything together
67. exist

2 CROSSWORD—WORDS OF LAUGHTER

Answers on page—117

2 CROSSWORD—WORDS OF LAUGHTER

ACROSS
1. a buttock and a small bread
3. 2nd of 2 words with 50 down—hip tease
5. a fancy smancy term for boobs
8. theoretical
10. ___ di da
11. favorite dyke creature
13. last name of a closet tv cop
14. lesbian with a boyfriend
15. Dorothy's Auntie ___
17. the vehicle of choice for the student
18. nibbled—a small piece
21. a kind of music
22. second of 2 words with 21 down — a young athletic girl with potential
23. lesbian bra
25. love potion
26. How we are likely to breath when we are in love
27. remove evidence of proclivities from a lesbian home
28. second of 2 words with 1 and 5 down — the time of year to switch lovers
31. not the opposite of go
33. _____ and Andy
35. a kind of sexy stockings
36. falling in intense like
38. Gertrude Stein's favorite euphemism
39. ___ in the clouds
42. early on when a worn path is made from the bed to the fridge- 2 words
45. she's perfect
46. a turn on in the video, *Erotic in Nature*
48. that of which every woman has two sets
51. lesbian summer cottage
53. she doesn't want to, once excited
54. who is it that runs into you for the rest of your life—2 words
56. what both cakes &lovers should be
60. Lesbian cruise ships
61. take to the breast
63. very heavy
64. New York (abbr.)
65. a no no

DOWN
1. 2nd half of the first of 2 words with 5 down and 28 across — time to switch lovers
2. _____ girls don't ....
4. she is celibate on principle
5. first 1/2 of 2 words with 1 down and 28 across—time of year to switch lovers
6. what it's all about
7. an ancient aphrodisiacal honey wine
9. the woman who loves women who wear aftershave
10. 2 words — affection for a synthetic
12. 2 words—helping to take off her Levis
14. two — prefix
16. what every woman is until she has made love to a woman
17. a woman who wears aftershave
18. The commericals warned us about it
19. career choice of a young lesbian— 2 words
20. a lesbian carpenter
21. first of 2 words with 22 across— a young athletic girl with potential
24. "The Amazon and the _____"
26. a signal for help
29. romantic orb—2 words
30. in order to reap you have to have....
32. the one and only
34. singing with your mouth closed
37. 2 words— the room we tell straight people belongs to our roommate, is one
40. a lesbian dinner for more than eight people
41. a small bite
43. making love at your place
44. what we sometime do after making love
49. Red_____ some dykes like to watch them
50. first of 2 words with 3 across—hip tease
52. go to her place
53. alternative spelling for lesbian
54. give me more
55. lesbians' favorite detective
57. also produces intense heat
58. if at first you don't succeed....
59. word that joins 2 women together
62. what we don't want our lovers to do

3 CROSSWORD—ENTERTAINMENT

Answers on page—117

#3 CROSSWORD—ENTERTAINMENT

ACROSS

1. this music keeps getting harder
4. author of the lesbian play *Last Summer at Bluefish Cove*
14. most feel it first time on stage
15. Hollywood is near this city (abbr.)
16. to look into
17. performers need to have_____
18. to play the part (two words)
20. dyke record company
23. day of the week (abr.)
24. another meaning for act
25. opinion feared of critics
26. what happened to all our good tapes
27. first name of popular lesbian singer _____ Bishop
29. to forgive is divine, to____ is human
32. as in a Jane Rule novel
35. practice
38. a greeting
39. you need a good one to succeed as a musician
40. she starred in *The Philadelphia Story*
43. the subway in Chicago
45. what we give for good entertainment
49. a woman who tries to keep us laughing
52. an island in Indonesia known for its artistry and dancing
54. *yes* in Spanish
55. the twenties was the _____ of ragtime
56. a woman's name in Nicaragua
57. the storyline
58. _____ *coming down* (in Holly Near's and Meg Christian's song).
59. A 1950's classic film _____ *Hur*
60. Singer Peggy ____
61. she became famous as a telephone operator on TV's *Laugh-in*
62. A negative
63. a lesbian performer, and a friend of Cris
66. how she responds (two words)
69. "*on a clear day you can___ forever*"
70. home entertainment
72. _____ Bernhardt, a great actress
74. illuminates the stage
77. "You can't always get what you want, but...you may just get what you ____"
78. an instrument found in churches —2 words
80. *Leaping Lesbian* woman
84. tells us about the play
85. ___and so
86. all of it
87. affirmative

DOWN

1. put on disk
2. popular these days for breakfast
3. bed for a baby
5. everything
6. it holds it together
7. it won't pay for the price of admission
8. tells us what play or movies are coming
9. some actors use it
10. a color often sung about
11. she played Our Miss Brooks, and many other roles in movies and TV
12. relax
13. Judy Garland starred in the film classic *A_____ Is Born.*
14. disappear from the screen
19. every dyke has one in her car
21. a 1987 movie about a woman who felt she was a man
22. in place
28. Holly Near's first major musical
30. performers have to pay it too
31. dancers tend to be this way
33. a word that means *esta* in Spanish
34. always cast as the same character
36. Egyptian god
37. The first name of the woman who wrote *The Children's Hour*
40. a funny dyke
41. performers often have a large one
42. both plays and women do it
44. she sings and plays an incredible fiddle
46. where all the famous people go to ski
47. nothing
48. unchanging plays (two words)
49. what one needs to be to go on stage
50. celluloid entertainment
51. two words — a performer's coiffeur
52. an exclamation of disapproval
53. not the truth
56. title for a man
63. on the way
64. "_____ *for Two....*"
65. famous lesbian singer
67. label
68. tit for ____
71. dip the head
73. let's play some _____
74. an actress must_____ her part
75. agents usually arrange to get this done
76. abbre. for system
79. an archaic negative
81. performers are always on the_____
82. to be included
83. ____ "*a meal with jam and bread*"

More Fill In The Bubbles

THE LESBIAN BOOK OF QUESTIONS

Dr. Wilhemmina Dyke, renowned lesbian psychotherapist and author of *The Bike Path Less Traveled, Women Who Love Women Too Much, Finally Out on a Limb,* and *No Bad Lesbians* has compiled a *Book of Questions* specifically designed to meet the needs of lesbians everywhere. Consider one or more of these questions during solitary reflection as a way of gaining insights into your own thoughts and beliefs. Or ask one with whom you resonate as many of the questions as possible to help make moving in with her a little less frightening. Pose these questions in a group situation to stimulate a lively exchange of ideas and values and thereby learn more about your softball buddies, book group gurus, or potluck lovers.

1) Would you move to a foreign country to live with a lover, even if that meant being cut off from your friends, family members, and a pool table for at least a year?

2) If a beautiful baby were left on your doorstep one morning, would your maternal instincts kick in or would you call one of your straight friends and tell her you finally got her a birthday present?

3) Would you rather sleep with your high school softball coach or the coach of your current softball team?

4) If you had the power to kill just by looking at a person and you were invited to a party that included all your ex-lovers, how many people would survive the night?

5) Describe what a "perfect date" would be like.

6) Would you rather have a successful career and lots of money but no life partner, or just get by financially and professionally but with a life partner?

7) While you're out of town, your lover has a one-night stand with another woman. Should she tell you about it? If the situation were reversed, would you tell her about it?

8) If you could wake up tomorrow and be the sexy, sensuous person you always wanted to be, in what ways would you be different?

9) What is your most enjoyable fantasy?

10) Do your lovers tend to be older than you or younger than you? Why?

11) Which would you rather do: perform a strip tease in front of a group of lesbians you don't know or ride naked on a motorcycle down the main street in your town?

12) If you could choose anyone as your lover, who would she be?

13) If you could rewrite your coming out experience, how would it be different?

14) Would you like it if your lover were not only more attractive and more intelligent than you, but also a better softball player?

15) Would you give up sex for a year if you could sleep with whomever you wanted when the year was up?

16) If scientists discovered a "cure" for rapists that would prevent them from raping again but, as a side effect, might also kill them, would you vote for its use?

17) Can you masturbate in front of another person?

18) Have you ever lied to an ex-lover? About what?

19) What female body part turns you on the most?

20) Are you in love with your therapist?

21) Imagine you could design a float for this year's gay pride march that would symbolize who you are and what you believe in. Describe the float.

22) Describe a tattoo you would like to have.

23) What have you done with material things (jewelry, clothes, etc.) given you by exs?

24) Describe the "perfect breakup."

25) Which is more physically arousing: playing one-on-one basketball with a woman you're attracted to or having an intimate conversation on a walk through the woods with someone you're attracted to?

26) Describe your ideal vacation.

27) Which dishes are you most likely to try at a pot luck: unidentifiable ones made by your friends or identifiable ones made by newcomers?

28) If you could live in any time period, when would you choose? Describe who you are and what you do.

29) Describe the most embarrassing moment of your life.

30) What would you do if your mother told you she was in love with a woman?

31) Would you like to know now whether or not you'll be in a long-term love relationship when you're forty? fifty? sixty? seventy?

32) What is your most disgusting personal hygiene habit?

33) Your lover and you have just argued. You are right and she is wrong, but she won't budge from her position and won't talk to you. How long would you wait before you talk to her? What will you do if she won't make up with you?

34) Have you ever lied to someone to break a date? What happened?

35) What is the quality you rate highest in a lover?

36) If women would pay to sleep with you, would you accept the money?

37) How would you dress if you wanted to look sexy?

38) Which type of nonfiction book would you purchase from a women's book store? Which type of fiction book?

39) If you could start any business you could that would help other lesbians, what would it be?

40) You are nominated to a highly visible political office. Would you come out?

41) If you could meet any woman author, living or dead, and tell her what her writing means to you, whom would you choose? What would you say?

42) Would you choose to be blind, deaf, or straight?

43) When was the last time you didn't take a close friend's advice? What happened?

44) Would you bail out a close friend from jail even if she wouldn't tell you what she did?

45) Imagine you are attracted to a sixteen-year-old girl. She is equally attracted to you. Would you act on your attractions?

46) If *Guinness Book of World Records* would pay you $100,000 to sleep with ten women in one night you don't know, would you do it?

47) Your mother accidentally stumbles across one of your mini vibrators and asks you what it is. What do you tell her?

48) Imagine you and your first lover could get back together. What would you want to do differently or be different from the first time?

49) In your opinion, what is the funniest thing about being a lesbian?

50) If you died a heroine-ic lesbian death, describe what it would be like.

LOCATE THE LESBIAN

LET'S BE HONEST, GIRLS....

#1. REVENGE IS SWEET

Your lover has broken up with you. The circumstances have been less-than-pleasant; you're mad as hell—and don't want to take it anymore.

Let's be honest. Do you want to do some of the revengeful things on the list below? Have you done these things before? If you can think of other acts of revenge that aren't on the list, feel free to add them.

1. Surround your ex- and her current lover with oodles of negative energy.

2. Throw her personal possessions on the front lawn or hold a yard sale.

3. Tear her love letters into teeny-tiny pieces, toss them into the blender, mix them at high speed for 2 minutes, then set fire to the mixture.

4. Repeatedly call her new telephone number in the middle of the night and, when she answers, hang up.

5. Join another softball team in the league—the one that came in first place last summer.

6 Gladly furnish credit collection agencies with her new address and telephone number.

Add your own...

7. _____

8. _____

9. _____

10 _____

11. _____

12. _____

MORE LET'S BE HONEST, GIRLS...

#2. THE GREAT LINES

You're at the dating stage in your relationships. How many times have you heard the following great lines—or given them to someone else? If you can think of other great lines, feel free to add them to the list.

1. You're the first person to ever make me feel this way.

2. I don't usually go to bed this quickly with someone.

3. You can always trust what I tell you.

4. I'm fully recovered from my break-up.

5. I'm not a jealous person. I don't mind if you go out with your friends or an ex.

6. My house/apartment usually doesn't look like this. Ordinarily I'm a very neat, organized person.

7. I'll call you soon.

Add your own...

8. _____

9. _____

10. _____

11. _____

12. _____

13. _____

The Lesbian Zodiac Revealed

Now, for the first time, a renowned feminist astrologer reveals the secrets of the zodiac as they apply to lesbians. Imogene Carlotta Stars, or I. C. Stars as she is known to those who call her 900 number and pay 95 cents for the first minute to hear their daily astrological forecasts, is the only astrologer to make the connection between celestial movements and their direct effect upon the lesbian population.

"So many lesbians consulted me about their future lives and their relationships that I knew I had come across a lucrative way to cash in on the current New Age craze," she explains. "I'd get a call like, 'I. C., I'm into S/M and just met this straight woman who's exploring her sexuality and so I went to a bisexual women's meeting with her and now she wants to know about coming out and coming in general and I don't know what I should do. She's a Capricorn and I'm an Aries. Can you help me?' Or I'd get another call: 'I. C., I'm a Sagittarius who's been in a long-term relationship with a Libra. All her previous lovers have been Leos, and sometimes she uses that as an excuse to avoid working out our problems. Lately a Gemini has been calling our house, then hanging up when I answer. What in the stars is going on?'"

Because of the flood of lesbian astrological calls she received, I. C. Stars left her 900 number callers on hold for a week while she researched and compiled her book, *SISTERS AND THE STARS: Lesbian Luck and Love in the Zodiac*. What follows are excerpts from this latest work.

ARIES

March 21—April 20

Symbol: the Ram

Element: fire

Favorite Place: Los Angeles, home of NFL's Rams

Rising Sign: She lowers her head and butts the alarm clock off the nightstand.

Ruling Food: any kind of grain

Qualities: Assertive and courageous; boldly goes where others have not gone before.

Abilities: to lead and dominate; to be on top of things, so to speak

The Aries lesbian comes from a long line of pioneers and explorers. Because of this, she's usually willing to take risks her friends wouldn't normally take; for example, walking into a San Francisco leather bar and saying to the toughest-looking dyke she meets, "Say, I'm new in town and don't know much about this leather stuff, but I'm certainly willing to explore."

Her symbol is the Ram, which has long been known as the sacrificial animal. Because of this, the Aries lesbian has a strong sense of self-preservation. She may take every self-defense course she can and often carries mace in her car. Symbolically, plants ruled by the Aries sign include garlic, peppers, onions, and nettle, which have a way of providing distance between themselves and others.

In a relationship the Aries lesbian finds monogamy a dull concept. She will tell you commitment may be good for others, but not for her. Her pioneer spirit loves new beginnings, so she always keeps her bags packed and an extra toothbrush handy to take off whenever she feels the urge to explore new territory. However, she is particularly compatible with fire signs Leo and Sagittarius and air signs Gemini, Libra, and Aquarius, which help keep her fires of passion burning.

If you want to hang onto an Aries lesbian, stay one step ahead of her. Be like Scheherazade, who prevented her death by telling one thousand and one tales of suspense and adventure: maintain the promise of more intense passion and even greater excitement in a relationship with you, but never give her everything you've got. Think of yourself as uncharted territory, and let her be the explorer!

April 21—May 20

Symbol: the Bull

Element: earth

Favorite Place: any arena

Rising Sign: She opens her eyes, snorts, then glares at you.

Ruling Food: anything red or, for that matter, anyone who wears red

Qualities: materialistic and pushy

Abilities: to bully others; to bullshit her way through things

TAURUS

In the olden days, a Taurus was often a farmer or builder of houses and was very connected to the land. Today's Taurus lesbian may still be connected to the land, but in a much different sense. Because of her materialistic tendencies, she is often bonded to the expensive luxuries in life that are usually found in earth's many shopping centers: possessions such as CDs, ATVs, VCRs, BMWs, and other groupings of alphabet letters that are valued in the thousands of dollars. The Taurus lesbian is also extremely protective of her wealth and valuable objects, so don't mess with this woman's CD player and never, ever ask to borrow her car!

Her symbol is the Bull; a plant ruled by her sign is spinach. This means that her focus is often on the brute power she can exert over people, places, and things like free weights, automobiles, and unyielding pickle jar covers. If she is striving to attain a personal goal, the Taurus lesbian will apply her bullish strength and not give up until she gets what she wants. However, if she is asked to do something out of her realm of personal gain or profit, her annoying bullish quality of stubbornness is likely to surface. During those times, she will plant both feet firmly on the ground and refuse to budge.

The Taurus lesbian is particularly compatible with Virgo and Capricorn, earth signs, and the water signs of Cancer, Scorpio, and Pisces. Her relationships are rarely based on quick assessments; rather, she forms alliances slowly and with determination. Once committed to a lover, however, she can be steadfast and loyal, although as stubborn as all hell when it comes to putting the cap back on the toothpaste tube or taking out the trash.

But the Taurus lesbian can change her heart's desire if she finds herself stimulated by another woman. When that happens—watch out! The Bull will charge full speed ahead and not be turned back by any matador!

GEMINI

May 21—June 20

Symbol: the Twins

Element: air

Favorite Place: the twin cities of Minneapolis and St. Paul

Rising Sign: She reads both Ann Landers and Dear Abby over her morning cup of coffee.

Ruling Food: Twinkies, Twix, or any food that's packaged in pairs

Qualities: nervous and excitable

Abilities: to be two people at the same time without being perceived as schizophrenic

The Gemini lesbian is like one of the actresses in a Doublemint gum advertisement: since she's under the sign of the twin, she'll try to find the double pleasures in life that are waiting for her. A menage a trois, therefore, is well within her realm of possibilities for a hot time in the city.

The Gemini lesbian is eager to experience life and love, sometimes to excess. She can usually be seen with a GAIA guidebook in her back pocket whenever she travels, just in case there's a bar or coffeehouse where she can check out the scene. She reads all the gay newspapers and often attends coming out workshops so she can get to know firsthand the new faces in town. And she never goes out on a Saturday night without a rubber dam in her wallet. In sum, the Gemini lesbian credo is "variety is the spice of life." And she likes her life very, very spicy!

The Gemini lesbian's theme song could easily be "Girls Just Wanna Have Fun" because to her, life should be all play and little work. Her ideal job is one where work comprises two weeks of the year and vacation makes up the rest of the time. Many Gemini lesbians wish they had the option of being a year-round lifeguard on the beaches near Provincetown or often fantasize ways of earning money while playing in softball tournaments across the country.

Just as the Gemini lesbian likes to view life as a playground, so too does she like to view her relationships. In her relationships, the Gemini lesbian is blessed with a strength of tongue, known as a great communicator who can discuss a wide array of subjects while, at the same time, deftly avoiding any intimate discussion of feelings.

As a result, the Gemini's partner rarely notices that she has uncovered very little about her Gemini love. Rather, she just lies back and experiences the gift of such a wonderful tongue!

June 21—July 22

Symbol: the Crab

Element: water

Favorite Place: the beach

Rising Sign: She'll pinch you to see if you're awake too.

Ruling Food: all seafood, except for other crabs

Qualities: can be extremely shellfish

Abilities: She can easily negotiate through crowded shopping malls and sidewalks by walking sideways

The Cancer lesbian's favorite jewelry is a string of pearls; she loves wearing shades of sea green and listening to the Paul Winter Consort's mammalian music. Even today, she may harbor the desire to sell seashells by the seashore. Her favorite soap is Coast. She always roots for Navy to win their football games against Army. She rates tropical fish way above cats or dogs as the perfect pets!

CANCER

Cancer is a maternal sign. Not surprisingly, the pictograph symbol for Cancer is breasts. In most Cancerian lesbians, the mammaries are quite large and full and ache to nourish most of the female world, especially on a Saturday night. Cancer lesbians often report a recurrent dream they have, of an endless line of lesbians waiting to place their mouths upon their breasts. Cancer lesbians desperately want to believe that "Life Sucks."

Cancer lesbians are extremely possessive of their lovers, and this never-let-go quality can make loving a Cancer in the highly social lesbian world quite difficult. (There's the story about a softball game in which a Cancer and her lover played the outfield for the same team. The Cancer thought her lover was attracted to a woman up at bat, who hit a fly ball deep into center field. When the Cancer saw her lover chasing after the woman's ball, her emotions got the best of her. She caught up to her lover, tackled her, and wouldn't let her near the ball. The right fielder eventually retrieved the ball and desperately threw it home; but alas, the game was lost.)

Yet the Cancer lesbian can provide hours of fun and frolic in a relationship. She's a great dancer, easily skittering to and fro on the dance floor as if she had eight legs. She loves to go to the beach and can expertly bury herself in the sand in a matter of minutes. And she loves to make love in the shower, taking to the warm, moist environment as easily as, well, a crab to water. To her, it's the perfect place in which to experience the taste o' the sea!

LEO

July 23—August 22

Symbol: The Lion

Element: Fire

Favorite Place: where other pussies hang out

Rising Sign: She'll let out one great big roar as she shows her awesome teeth and ample claws.

Ruling Food: meat—any kind

Qualities: self-assured, brave, courageous, protective of any woman named Dorothy

Ability: to lick a woman from head to toe without choking on an errant hair

Historically, the Leo lesbian comes from a long line of commanders and rulers. As a result, she can have the passion of Cleopatra, the fearlessness of Joan of Arc, the vindictiveness of Marie Antoinette, the intelligence of Marie Curie, the persistence of Harriet Tubman, the spiritual strength of Indira Ghandi, and the athletic prowess of Babe Didrickson. In sum, the Leo lesbian is one hell of a woman!

A Leo commands attention, no matter what her occupation. As long as she's in charge (take note, "Tops" who have the hots for a Leo) or all eyes are focused on her, she's happy. She's the ultimate performer who believes life's the stage upon which she's the star. She loves to be watched; hand her a vibrator, for example, and shine a Black and Decker spotlighter on her, and she'll give you a performance that'll put cream in your coffee! But while she craves the undivided attention and complete admiration from others, she also likes to keep herself at a distance until she gets to know you. So the key word is "resist" when you find yourself attracted to the Leo lesbian. Move too fast on her, and you're likely to get your face scratched!

But while the Leo lesbian may be a ferocious feline in most situations, in affairs of the heart she often turns into a housecat that craves attention and affection. Leos love to be wooed and cooed, cuddled and snuggled, and pampered with fancy feasts. While they are most compatible with the fire signs of Aries and Sagittarius and air signs Gemini, Libra, and Aquarius, Leos will rub up against the legs of any woman who knows exactly where to scratch them!

August 23—Sept. 22

Symbol: the Virgin

Element: earth

Favorite Place: home, where she keeps her heart (and more) under lock and key

Rising Sign: She consults her horoscope to see if this is the day she'll meet the love of her life.

Ruling Food: anything wholesome from the four food groups

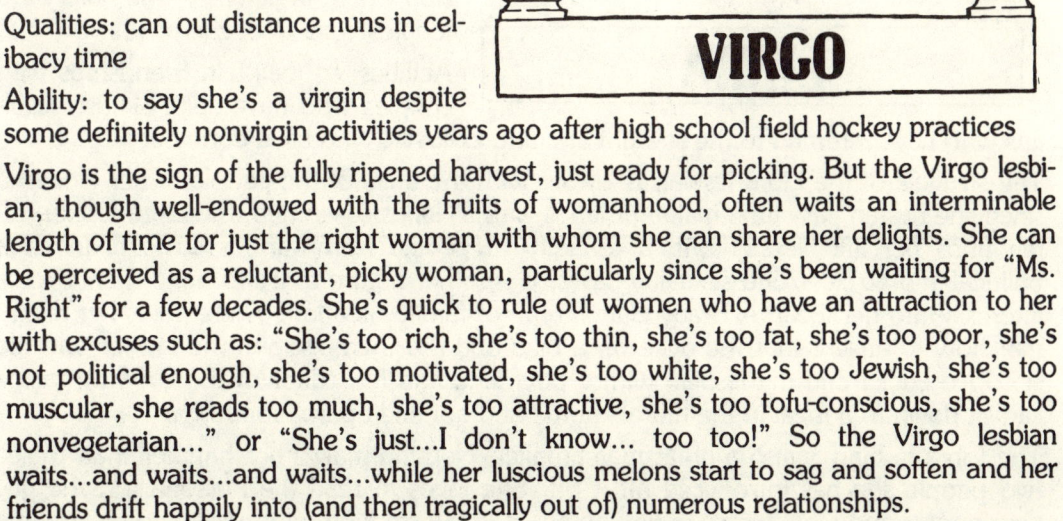

Qualities: can out distance nuns in celibacy time

Ability: to say she's a virgin despite some definitely nonvirgin activities years ago after high school field hockey practices

VIRGO

Virgo is the sign of the fully ripened harvest, just ready for picking. But the Virgo lesbian, though well-endowed with the fruits of womanhood, often waits an interminable length of time for just the right woman with whom she can share her delights. She can be perceived as a reluctant, picky woman, particularly since she's been waiting for "Ms. Right" for a few decades. She's quick to rule out women who have an attraction to her with excuses such as: "She's too rich, she's too thin, she's too fat, she's too poor, she's not political enough, she's too motivated, she's too white, she's too Jewish, she's too muscular, she reads too much, she's too attractive, she's too tofu-conscious, she's too nonvegetarian..." or "She's just...I don't know... too too!" So the Virgo lesbian waits...and waits...and waits...while her luscious melons start to sag and soften and her friends drift happily into (and then tragically out of) numerous relationships.

But while the Virgo lesbian's sexuality may seem to be perpetually on hold, the Virgo's mind is quite active. Because of this, Virgo lesbians are the people to organize social groups for any persuasion (a support group for left-handed Lithuanian lesbians addicted to amusement park rides) or popular women's events that require hours of hair-pulling in order to achieve success. Leave everything up to the highly organized Virgo lesbian, and she'll design and print the fliers, determine the number and variety of workshops, supervise the kitchen help as they prepare a spread of politically correct foods, and select the best sites for the port-o-potties.

Virgo lesbians also make good softball team managers by keeping accurate team statistics and knowing the opposition's hitting abilities. They'll also be quick to note who's with whom on the social scene and, although they won't make a big issue out of it, will keep their eyes open just in case the one with "the right stuff" comes along!

LIBRA

Sept. 23—October 22

Symbol: the Scales

Element: air

Favorite Place: the produce section of any grocery store

Rising Sign: She'll weigh herself

Ruling Food: any food that's in measurable quantities (two ounces of cheese, a Quarter Pounder, a quarter teaspoon mayonnaise, etc.)

Qualities: to appear to make a decision when, in actuality, she hasn't the foggiest idea what she wants

Abilities: to maintain friendships with couples who have split, skittish lesbians who have returned to the straight life, and ex-lovers who have done her wrong.

The struggle of the Libra lesbian is always with the unity of the people in her life. And since she has an easy time making friends with all kinds of women, the Libra lesbian often finds her life blessed with a diversity of people from various socio/economic/political/moral/class/and sexuality bases. It is in her nature to try to unite such diverse interests into her ideal: A Brady Bunch type of family situation. Therein lies her dilemma: how to ensure that the dyke on a bike and the therapist and the lawyer and the sex/love addict and the lesbian with a boyfriend and the editor of the S/M magazine can sit down to a meal in the Libra's home and not end up in a food fight.

The Libra lesbian is also a great matchmaker. Nothing makes her happier than to see two people she has introduced hit it off. She loves to read the Personals in the gay newspapers and often writes to box numbers to inform them of other box numbers that might be of interest to them.

But after all her matchmaking and unifying is done and the Libra lesbian sits back to contemplate her wonderful work, she may suddenly come to the panicked realization that she's the only one who's sleeping alone. And the Libra lesbian hates to sleep alone. So she'll make a concerted effort to meet new people and, as typical of the Libra lesbian nature, she won't be alone for long.

But therein lies another Libran dilemma: when faced with the ultimatum to choose one woman with whom to settle down, the Libra lesbian is unable to make a choice. Rather, she'll push long and hard for nonmonogamy so she can have her cakes—and eat them, too!

Oct. 23—Nov. 22

Symbol: the Scorpion

Element: water

Favorite Place: inside people's shoes

Rising Sign: She'll give you a quick, stinging slap across your behind before heading to the shower.

Ruling Food: any spicy food with a bite to it

Qualities: uses friends for personal gain, seduces others for sexual pleasure, yet rises above these qualities and is known as a nice person

Abilities: to feel pleasure and pain at the same time and to enjoy them both equally

SCORPIO

While the Libra lesbian strives for unity of mind, the Scorpio lesbian strives for unity of the body—any body—with hers. Her theme song could easily be "I Want Your Sex." Her desire is for sexual merging through numerous sexual liaisons that take the guise of emotional relationships. The Scorpio lesbian's motto is: "I desire everyone and I don't care how I get them," despite the fact that she usually resonates with the water signs Cancer and Pisces and earth signs Taurus, Virgo, and Capricorn.

The Scorpio lesbian is a skilled seducer, using the hypnotic magnetism of her eyes to lure yet another into a sexual encounter. Not surprisingly, her sign is known to regulate the flow of sexual bodily fluids. So if you find yourself in a seductive stare-down with a woman and feel yourself becoming wetter than you've ever been before, know that you're probably caught in the clutches of a tenacious Scorpio. And accept that you'll probably not escape. She's so skilled at her seductive powers that even Cinderella would have had one more dance with her while the bells were chiming the midnight hour! The Scorpio lesbian is not only a skilled seducer, but an equally skilled lovemaker. Her sexual capabilities often leave her partners feeling like they've been injected with the poison from the sting of a scorpion: they're weak and immobile, in a near-death state where any more sexual activity would be overkill. It's then that the Scorpio lesbian crawls out of your bed and between the legs of her next prey!

SAGITTARIUS

November 23—December 21

Symbol: The Hunter or Archer

Element: fire

Favorite Place: any lesbian singles' hangout

Rising Sign: She'll throw a dart at an activity board to decide what her course of action for the day will be.

Ruling Food: politically correct meats such as tofu venison, tempeh buffalo wings, kashi kebobs, and bulgar burgers

Qualities: a great camping partner who always has a stack of firewood handy.

Abilities: to track down a lesbian in any crowd; to look great in a day-glo orange vest.

The Sagittarius lesbian can be a woman of many contradictions. Although she may be a vegetarian and an extremely passive individual, she may also have a handgun in her nightstand drawer and several issues of *Field and Stream* under her bed. Historically, Sagittarians have been avid sportsmen, so the Sagittarius lesbian often finds the babble of the trout stream and the quack of the airborne duck too hard to resist. When she does, she loads her Blazer with camping equipment, rifles, rounds of ammo, and rod and reel, and spends several days hunting, fishing, and chowing down all-natural meat. When this craving is satisfied, she returns to her apartment in the city and her job at the women's book store and resumes her normal routine of shopping at the local health food store, passing out anti-NRA fliers on the street corner, and picketing in front of the city's largest fur supplier.

The Sagittarius lesbian is often attracted to the fire signs Leo and Aries and air signs Gemini, Libra, and Aquarius. But this lesbian's sign is of the confirmed bachelorette. She'd rather have several uncommitted relationships going on at a time than one that would place restrictions upon her freedom. She's always on the hunt for a new babe; with her keen sense of smell, she can saunter into any bar or party and know which lesbian is ready for a hot time. But don't count on her to stay in one geographic area for too long. The Sagittarius lesbian is a restless and edgy woman. She'll set out for another hunting ground when she feels she's trapped all the "game" in one area or herself becomes the hunted!

December 22—January 19

Symbol: the Mountain Goat

Element: earth

Favorite Place: any height

Rising Sign: She'll bleat and chew on the bedsheets.

Ruling Food: any inedible object

Qualities: strong feet and hands

Abilities: to never look down from any height, even when friends are screaming, "Don't look down!"

The sign of the Mountain Goat can be seen as one of pessimism ("That damn mountain can't be climbed..."),

CAPRICORN

dogged perseverance ("By golly, I'm gonna climb it..."), and careful coolness ("But I'm not going to take any foolish chances when I do..."). Unlike the Aries Ram, who charges full speed ahead up the mountain and then wonders why she did it, the Capricorn lesbian undertakes nothing without careful thought and pragmatic consideration of its meaning to her life. Often this has good benefits—Capricorn lesbians can be shrewd stock investors and highly competitive game players. But sometimes such consideration can be seen as ploddingly slow, particularly when she's keeping a carload of people waiting as she considers whether going to P-town on the spur of the moment really suits her best interests. In the same vein, many Capricorn lesbians are not very good softball players; they are often called out on strikes at the plate because they can't make up their minds which pitch best serves their interests.

Those who interact with the Capricorn lesbian say that she is as aloof as the mountaintop she attains. "Power and mastery over others" is the Capricorn lesbian's motto; she loves to be in the position of authority and control. She's the cruiser, the asker-out, the maker of the first move in bed, the one on top, and the orderer of all the sex toys.

Because of this aloofness, the Capricorn lesbian's nature is to remain as uninvolved with people's lives as possible. Even in a relationship, she tries to remain as emotionally unattached as she can. Oftentimes she's oblivious to even the most obvious problems; it's not surprising, for example, for a Capricorn lesbian to be in a committed relationship on Tuesday night and wake up on Wednesday morning alone after her lover has given up trying to resolve issues for the umpteenth time.

But the Capricorn lesbian's feeling in such a situation may be: "Her loss; my gain," as she pragmatically resumes the search for another lover. There are always other mountains to climb!

AQUARIUS

January 20—February 19

Symbol: the Water Bearer

Element: air

Favorite Place: Haight-Ashbury

Rising Sign: She'll sing, at the top of her lungs, "Let the sun shine...let the sun shine in," as she dances naked around the bedroom.

Ruling Food: any really, really good organic food

Qualities: wants to give peace a chance (that's all she is saying)

Abilities: to apply the philosophy of the '60s to anything in her life

No matter what her age, the Aquarius lesbian loves the show "Family Ties," frequently uses the terms "radical" and "far out" as descriptive words, has a Nehru jacket hanging in her closet, drives a motorcycle because it's "a trip," and can't understand why Gloria Steinem had to change. She knows how to picket, sit in, groove, swing, rap, and protest. She's hip to what's happening, even if what's happening is so far out from her '60s perspective that she has a difficult time not tuning out to today's lesbian "establishment."

Aquarius is the sign of consciousness; the Aquarian lesbian has been trying to raise hers for years. Today she ponders the demise of coffeehouses and protest songs; she refuses to believe Janice Joplin had a drinking and drug problem; she contends that sleeping on a park bench is politically correct and not a national problem; she doesn't understand rap music or the New Jefferson Starship. Today's Aquarian lesbian strives very much to be in touch with the issues of the '80s, but items like safe sex still boggle her mind. In fact, when she first heard the term "rubber dam" she thought beavers had banded together to save the national forests!

While many of the lesbian interests of the '80s may be beyond her comprehension, the Aquarian lesbian is a humanitarian who strives for sisterhood. She believes strongly in the oneness of all lesbians and strives to garner interest in her ideal of a more perfect lesbian world. Her world is one based on a communal experience, where lesbians from all walks of life and all backgrounds can live together in peace and harmony off the land. She strongly believes in this ideal of shared labor, nonmaterialistic goals, and free love between all members. Thus far, free love is the only facet of her dream that's generated much interest.

February 20—March 20

Symbol: the Fish

Element: water

Favorite Place: any city aquarium

Rising Sign: She'll pucker her lips together and suck your face– and more!

Ruling Food: flaked food

Qualities: goes with the flow

Abilities: to hold her breath for really long periods of time; to deftly imitate Flipper's noises

PISCES

Pisces is the most powerful water sign of all the water signs in the zodiac; because of this, fluids play a great role in the Pisces lesbian's life. She may drink Lite beers like a fish, spend a great deal of time swimming laps at the Y, be the one appointed to bring the water jugs to the softball games, or own a large quantity of beverage stocks. But take away the security of fluids in her life, in whatever form, and she'll have a hard time going along with the flow.

The Pisces lesbian is a creative and imaginative individual who deals with the circumstances in her life in a few ways. If the situation is too much for her to handle, she can dive away from it. If an experience is pleasant or pleasurable, she can easily float along with it. If she desires something, she can swim towards it and grasp it. Even during the most storm-tossed situation, such as a heated argument with a lover or her book group's selection of next month's literature, the Pisces lesbian can easily float beneath the tempestuous surface and find peace and serenity while everyone else is battling to stay afloat in the sea of discontent.

In a love relationship, the Pisces lesbian is drawn towards water signs, Cancer and Scorpio and earth signs, Taurus, Virgo, and Capricorn. Although she may go to great lengths to avoid being caught in the nets of an all-consuming relationship, once she takes the bite, she's caught—hook, line, and sinker. Then the Pisces lesbian becomes like a barracuda, plunging into the wet waves of orgasmic delights that crash repeatedly upon her sensuous shores.

Afterwards, left gasping for air, she's one fish with a tale to tell!

Not so TRIVIA: Herstory

Answers —on page 115

1. Who wrote *Lesbian Nation?*

2. What French feminist wrote *The Lesbian Body?*

3. What famous lesbian had herself delivered to Renee Vivien in a box of lillies?

4. What feminist organizer and writer was in the TV show *I Remember Mama* as a teen-ager?

5. Who founded the feminist publishing Co. *Daughters Inc.?*

6. What book first published by Daughters Inc. became a Lesbian classic?

7. Name the civil rights activist who later came out as a lesbian.

8. What was the name of the publication of the Daughters of Bilitis?

9. What is the real name of the athlete who played in....*Personal Best?*

10. Who was reputed to be Virginia Woolfe's lesbian lover?

11. What did Gertrude Stein mean by the word cow in her writing?

12. Were there lesbians in the Stonewall gay bar when the police raided it and the patrons rebelled?

13. What was the name of the outspoken black civil rights and lesbian rights lawyer ?

14. Who wrote *Edward the Dyke?*

15. Where did the word dyke come from?

16. What famous hostess in prewar France was called the Amazon of Letters?

17. Who wrote the *SCUM Manifesto* and later was accused of shooting Andy Warhol?

18. Who replied to Phil Donahue's remark,"You don't look 40," with the rejoinder "This is what 40 looks like."

19. Who wrote the song, *Ode to a Gym Teacher?*

20. Who founded Naiad Press?

21. How many dykes does it take to screw in a lightbulb?

Connect the Dyke Answer

1) **Identification:** C - Social Worker

2) **Description:** A - Her head tilted empathically to one side and her long permed hair loose, demonstrating relaxed receptivity, she is inexpensively stylish in a funky sort of way. Her accessories include a kerchief around her neck, dangling earrings, and bangle bracelets. She wears oversized shirts tied with a sash, free flowing long skirts, wool socks, and Birkenstock sandals.

3) **Accoutrements:** G - A proverbial date book and a portable clock

4) **Habitat:** D - She is most often found at lectures, seminars, workshops (any place where CEUs can be obtained), and in the Juvenile Courts.

5) **Transportation:** H - She drives an economical yet functional Japanese car, complete with all the amenities.

6) **Common expressions:** C - The words most often out of her mouth are, "How do you feel about that?" and, "Thank you for sharing that with me."

7) **Last book read:** C - *Lesbian Psychologies*, edited by the Boston Lesbian Psychologies Collective

8) **Heroine:** F - Carol Gilligan, Jean Baker Miller, and all the blessed beings at the Stone Center.

9) **Social group or professional affiliation:** E - She joins support groups for lesbian therapists who are survivors of traditional clinical practice.

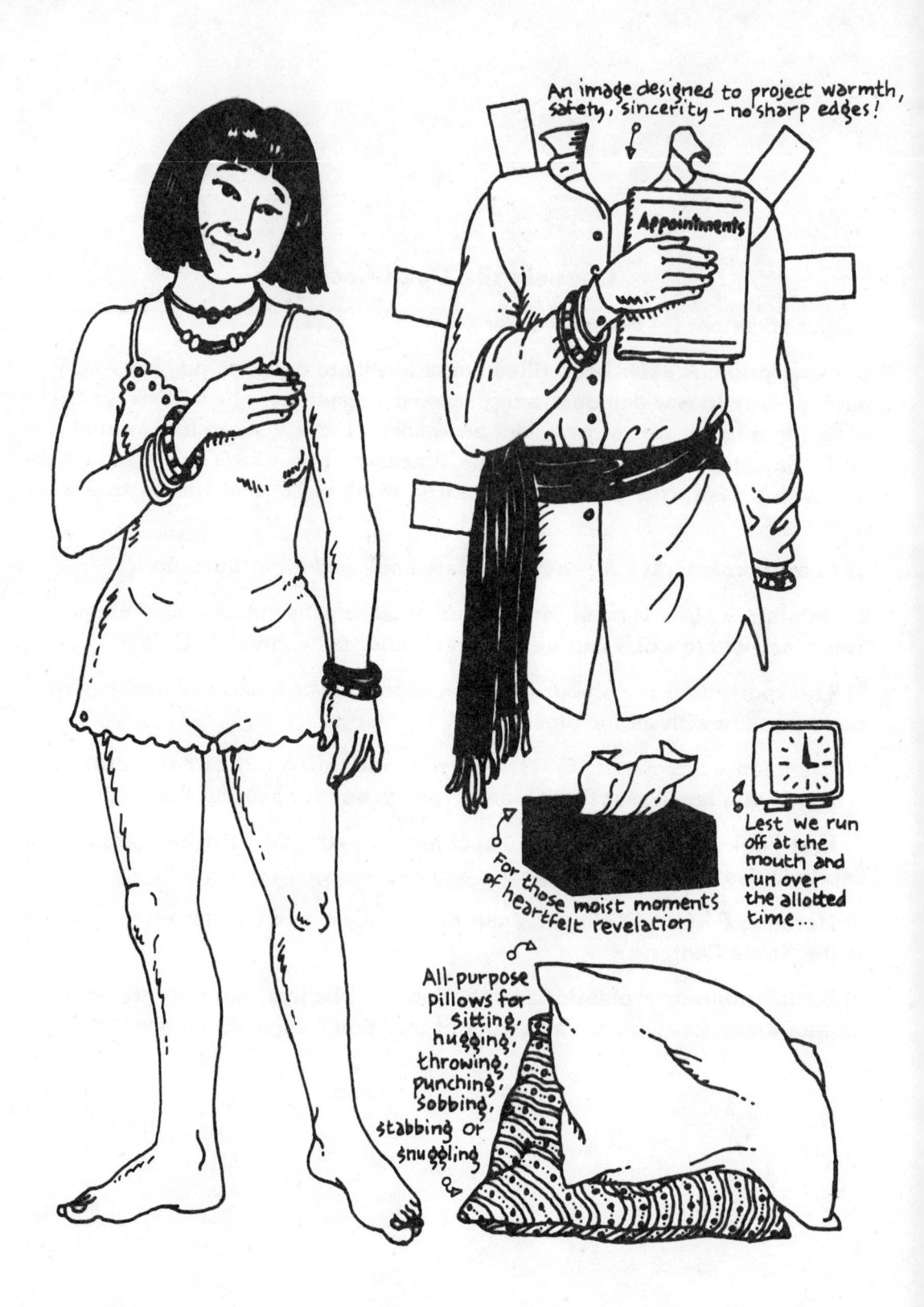

An image designed to project warmth, safety, sincerity — no sharp edges!

Appointments

For those moist moments of heartfelt revelation

Lest we run off at the mouth and run over the allotted time...

All-purpose pillows for sitting, hugging, throwing, punching, sobbing, stabbing or snuggling

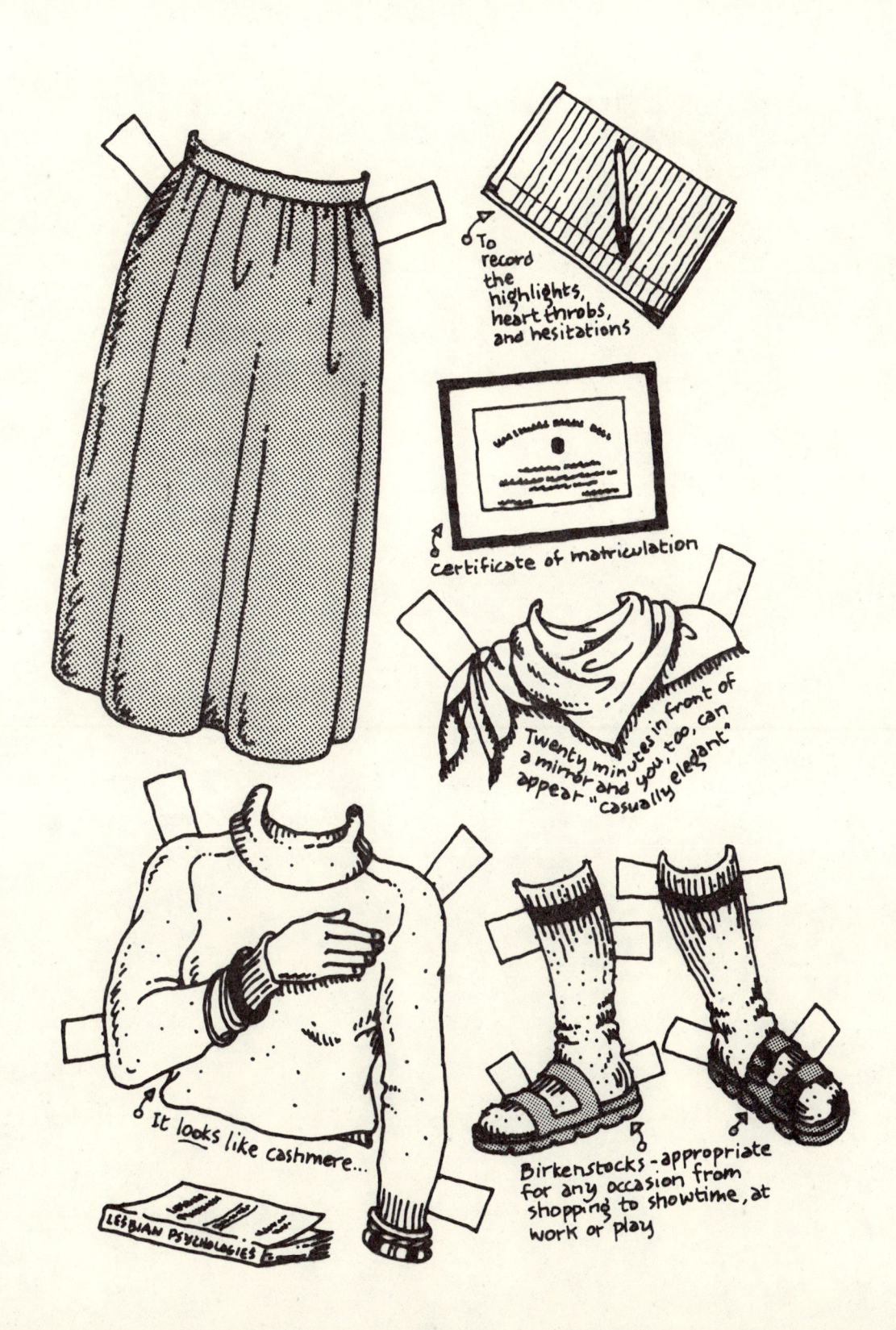

To record the highlights, heart throbs, and hesitations

certificate of matriculation

Twenty minutes in front of a mirror and you, too, can appear "casually elegant"

It looks like cashmere...

LESBIAN PSYCHOLOGIES

Birkenstocks - appropriate for any occasion from shopping to showtime, at work or play

Connect The Dyke answers

1) **Identification:** A - Don Juanita

2) **Description:** D - She's a smooth operator, dressed to the nines at every social occasion. Her moussed hair is brushed back from her face for that lean and hungry look. She adorns herself with long dangling earrings, a bracelet or two, and gold chains around her neck. She wears a high necked silk shirt under her double breasted evening jacket. Her stylish black pleated pants taper at the bottom over her shiny black pointed leather shoes.

3) **Accoutrements:** F - She is armed with a little black book and a cigarette lighter.

4) **Habitat:** G - She is found in bars, at softball games, potlucks, dances -- basically anyplace where lesbians are to be cruised (no event is too large or too small for a Cassanova lesbian).

5) **Transportation:** B - A red sports car (or at least a desire for one).

6) **Common expressions:** F - "Have we met before? Your eyes are so intense! What sign are you? I usually don't act this way with people I've just met, but....."

7) **Last book read:** H - *Lesbian Sex* and *Lesbian Passion*, by JoAnn Loulan, *Pleasures*, by Lonnie Barbach, The Joy Of Lesbian Sex, by Emily l. Sisley and Bertha Harris. ANYTHING, including the Dictionary and the Bible, as long as there is sex in it.

8) **Heroine:** G - Patricia Charboneau, star of *Desert Hearts*.

9) **Social group or professional affiliation:** A - She is involved in any group where there is potential for becoming involved with any of the group's members.

Makeup

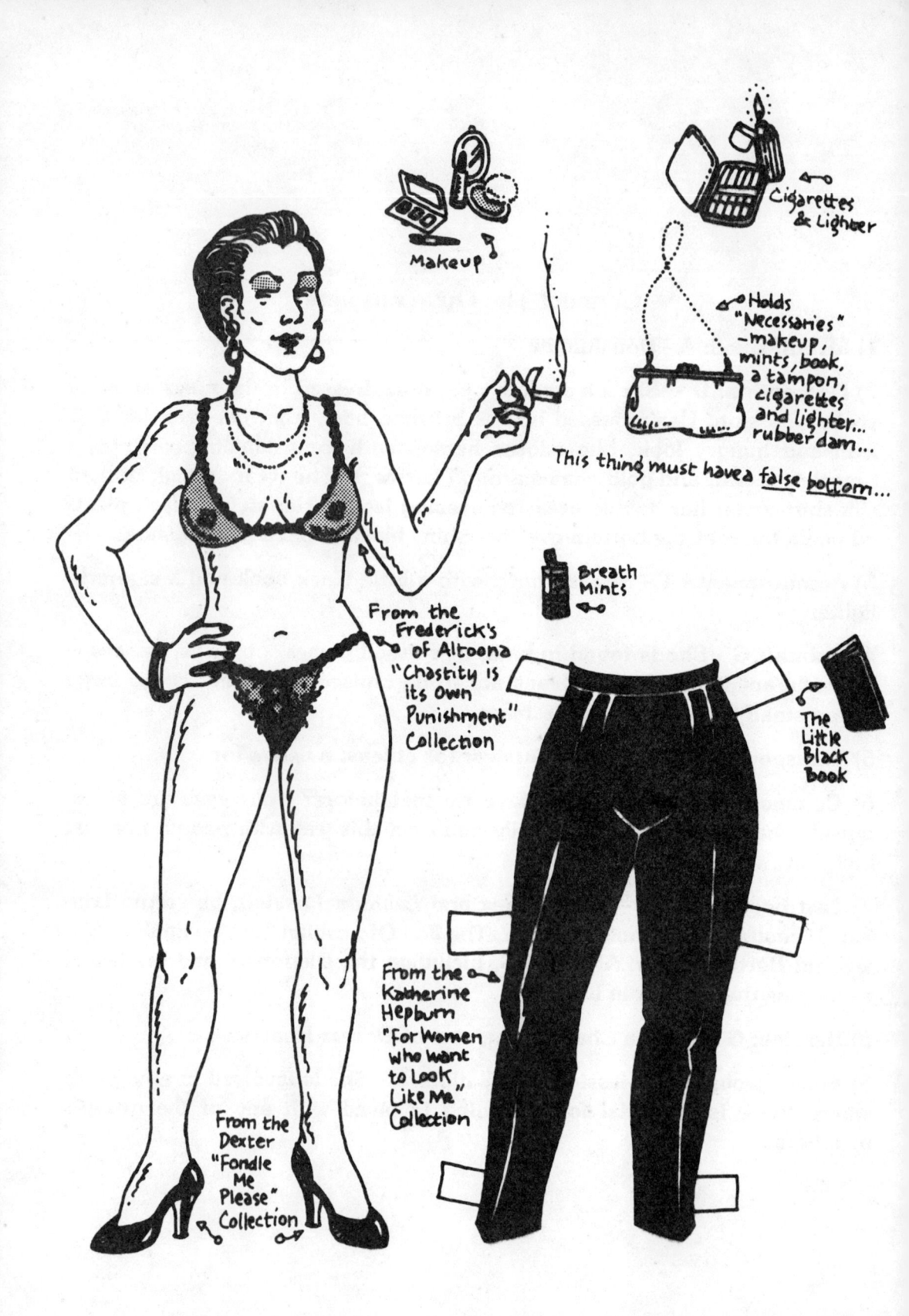

Cigarettes & Lighter

Holds "Necessaries" — makeup, mints, book, a tampon, cigarettes and lighter... rubber dam...

This thing must have a false bottom...

From the Frederick's of Altoona "Chastity is its Own Punishment" Collection

Breath Mints

The Little Black Book

From the Katherine Hepburn "For Women who Want to Look Like Me" Collection

From the Dexter "Fondle Me Please" Collection

From the Lauren Bacall "Key Largo" Collection

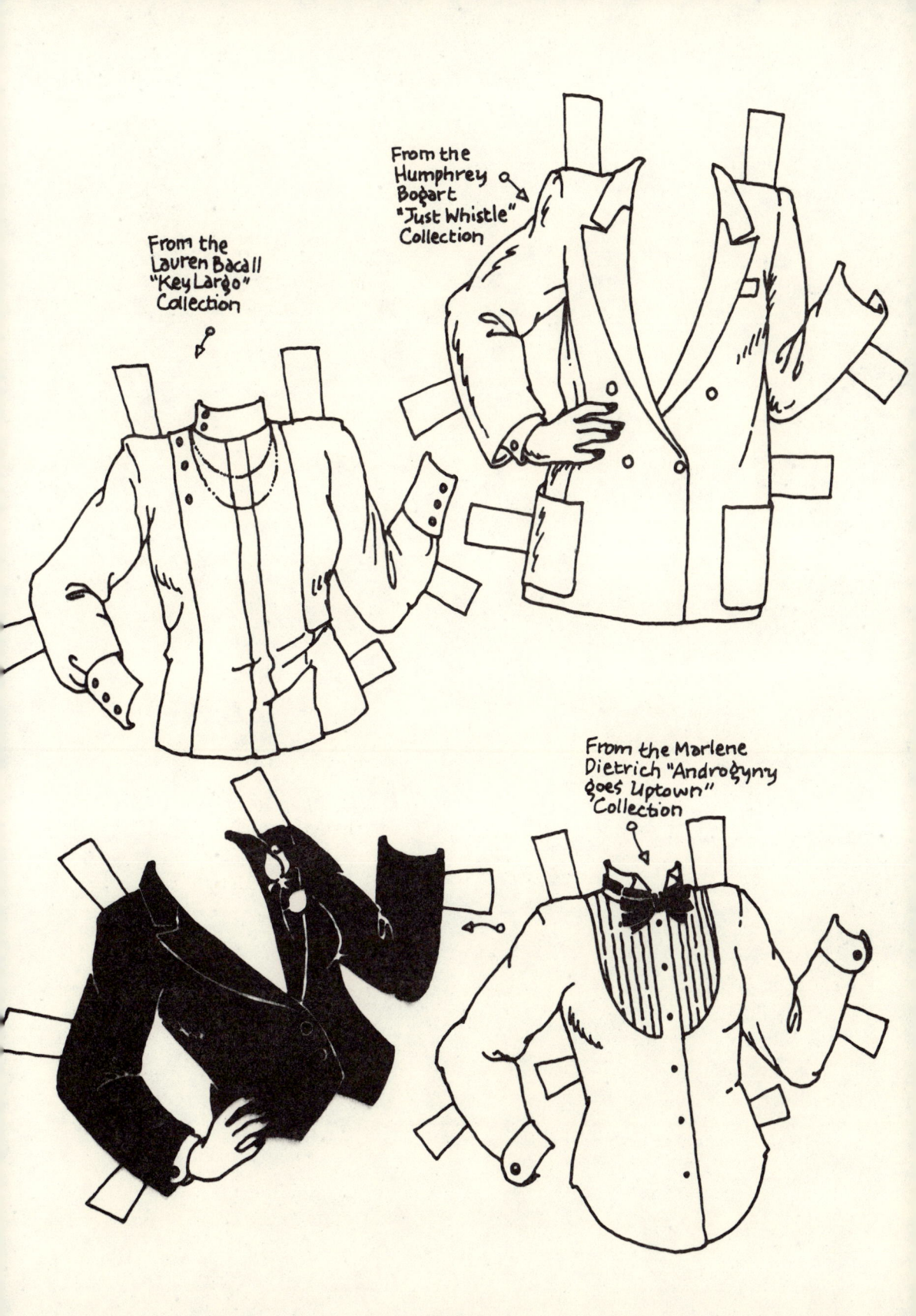

From the Humphrey Bogart "Just Whistle" Collection

From the Marlene Dietrich "Androgyny goes Uptown" Collection

Connect the Dyke answers

1) **Identification:** F - Timberdyke

2) **Description:** H - This strong and sturdy woman is usually found wearing a worn flannel shirt, tan steel-toed boots with woolen socks rolled over the tops, old jeans with holes at the knees exposing red long underwear, and a visored cap with John Deere imprinted on the front. Her face is perpetually tanned and weathered, with squint lines around her eyes from looking into the sun. She has a satisfied look on her face from having created things with her own hands

3) **Accoutrements:** B - Chainsaw optional.

4) **Habitat:** E - When not in the woods, this woman can be found in hardware stores or feed and grain stores early on a Saturday morning. She is also likely to be spotted anywhere that tractors or other large earth-moving equipment are found.

5) **Transportation:** C - An American made pick-up truck, battered but loved.

6) **Common expressions:** G - Besides terse comments about the weather, she is not likely to engage in idle coversation, especially while the sun is still up.

7) **Last book read:** A - The Time- Life Series on How to Build Your Own Outhouse.

8) **Heroine:** B - Annie Oakley and the spirit of the frontier women.

9) **Social group or professional affiliation:** G - Wilderness Women of Washington County

92

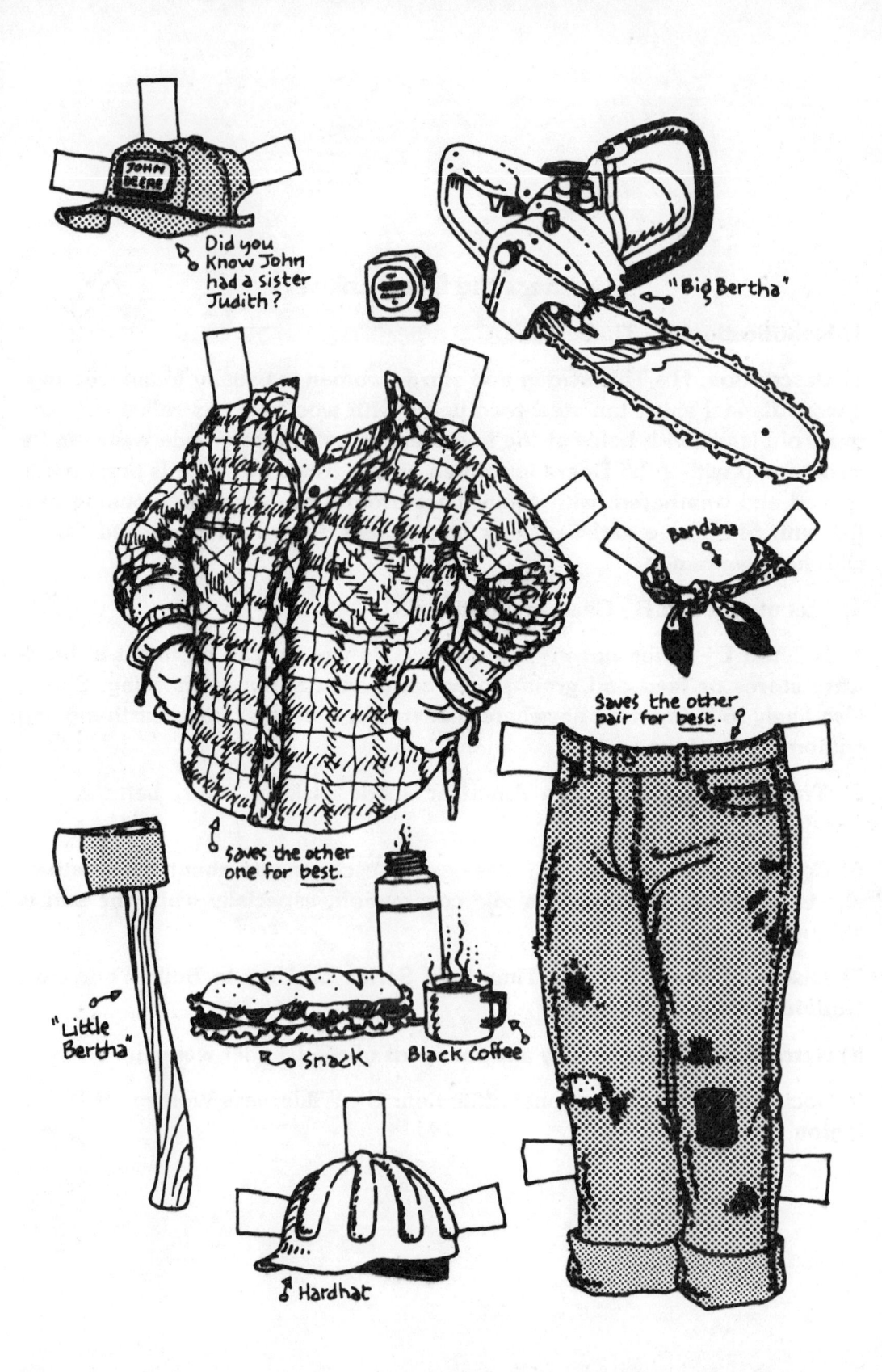

Come in Scarlet or white but the red ones always seem warmer.
Drop seat.

Waffle Stompers A.K.A. ShitKickers

BAG BALM

93

Connect the Dyke answers

1) Identification: E- Baby Dyke or Dykeling

2) Description: B - This young innocent is readily identified by her preppy-like boyish appearance, complete with button-down collar, pullover sweater, chinos, and deck shoes. She looks at her newly-discovered world with wide-eyed wonderment while keeping herself tightly under wraps.

3) Accoutrements: A - A calendar listing from the regional gay newspaper.

4) Habitat: C - She is found on college campuses, Cris Williamson concerts, or at any women's event anywhere.

5) Transportation: D - Her parents' car complete with college stickers, graduation tassels, and assorted toys on the dashboard

6) Common expressions: E - With the zealousness of a new convert, she proclaims sixties feminist rhetoric as her own.

7) Last book read: F - *Rubyfruit Jungle*, by Rita Mae Brown, because it is the only book she knows about.

8) Heroine: E - The heroine of *Rubyfruit Jungle*, by Rita Mae Brown.

9) Social group or professional affiliation: B - 25 and under lesbian rap groups.

Button-front Levi's

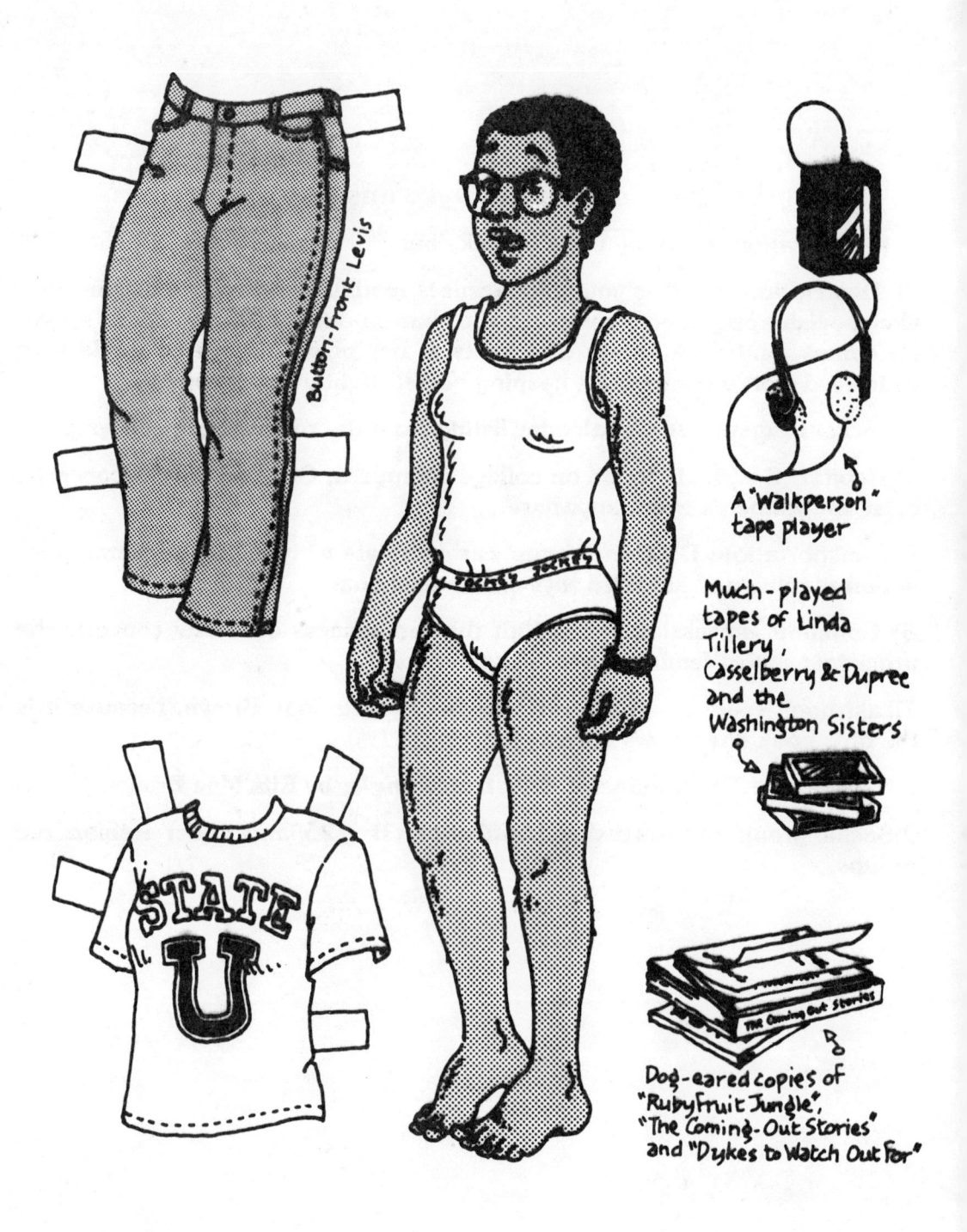

STATE U

A "Walkperson" tape player

Much-played tapes of Linda Tillery, Casselberry & Dupree and the Washington Sisters

Dog-eared copies of "Rubyfruit Jungle", "The Coming-Out Stories" and "Dykes to Watch Out For"

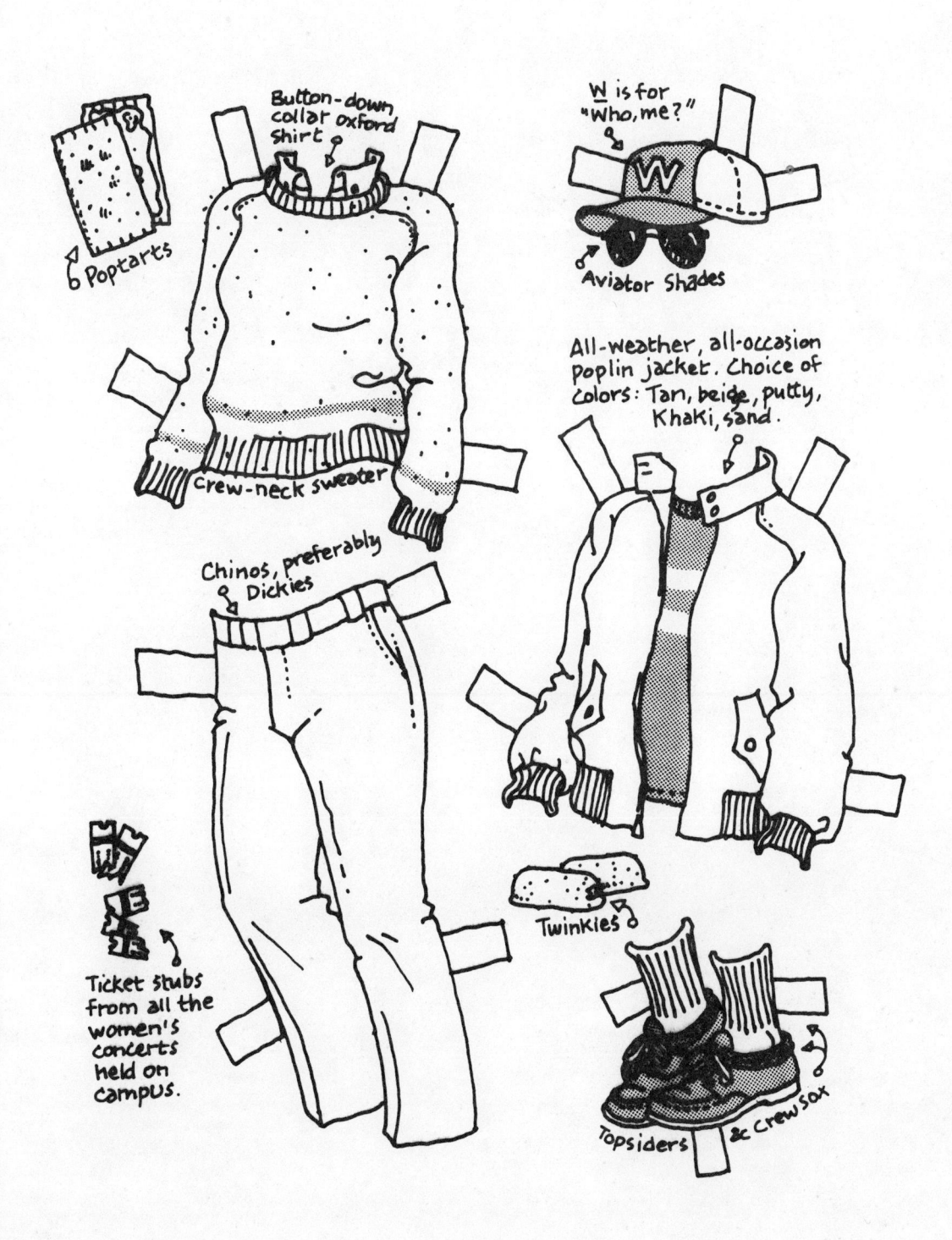

- Poptarts
- Button-down collar oxford shirt
- Crew-neck sweater
- W is for "Who, me?"
- Aviator Shades
- All-weather, all-occasion poplin jacket. Choice of colors: Tan, beige, putty, khaki, sand.
- Chinos, preferably Dickies
- Ticket stubs from all the women's concerts held on campus.
- Twinkies
- Topsiders & Crew Sox

Connect the Dyke Answer

1) Identification: D - Intelligentsia

2) Description: E - The self-proclaimed intellectual elite of the lesbian community, she controls her life through her "superior" reasoning powers and her ability to criticize everyone and everything. Her dress is conservative, usually well coordinated clothes from a discount department store. Social wear consists of a cotton blouse under a sweater, corduroys usually a bit too short, argyle socks, and sensible shoes. Formal wear would include a blazer.

3) Accoutrements: H - Always prepared with book, pens, notebooks and often computer paper.

4) Habitat: F - This type of lesbian's social highlight is the monthly book-club, where she has the opportunity to flex her intellectual biceps and, with her peers, reveals her profound insights into other people's writing.

5) Transportation: A - Any car that has been carefully researched and comparison priced so that the best value for the least money has been achieved.

6) Common expressions: B - The single most common word proclaimed by her is "But." As in, "I agree with you whole-heartedly but.... I know you are an expert in this field but...." Whatever the conversation, you can rest assured she will stick her "but" into it.

7) Last book read: E - The A-L section of the local library, alphabetically

8) Heroine: H - She does not have a heroine because she finds fault with everyone.

9) Social group or professional affiliation: F - The book club or any organization where her intellectual and critical skills can be utilized.

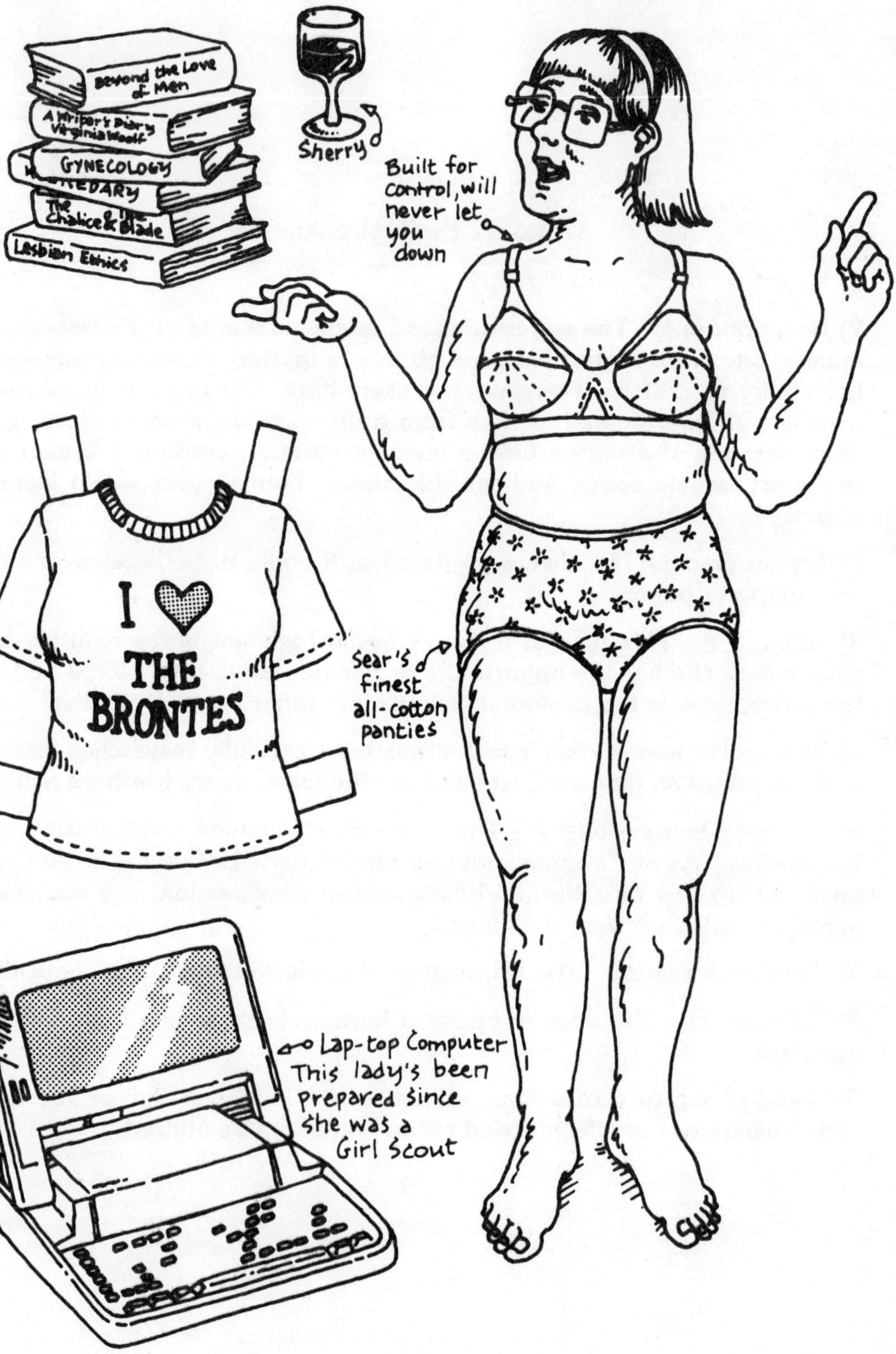
Beyond the Love of Men
A Writer's Diary Virginia Woolf
GYNECOLOGY
The Chalice & The Blade
Lesbian Ethics
Sherry
Built for control, will never let you down
I ♥ THE BRONTES
Sear's finest all-cotton panties
Lap-top Computer This lady's been prepared since she was a Girl Scout

Pocket Thesaurus

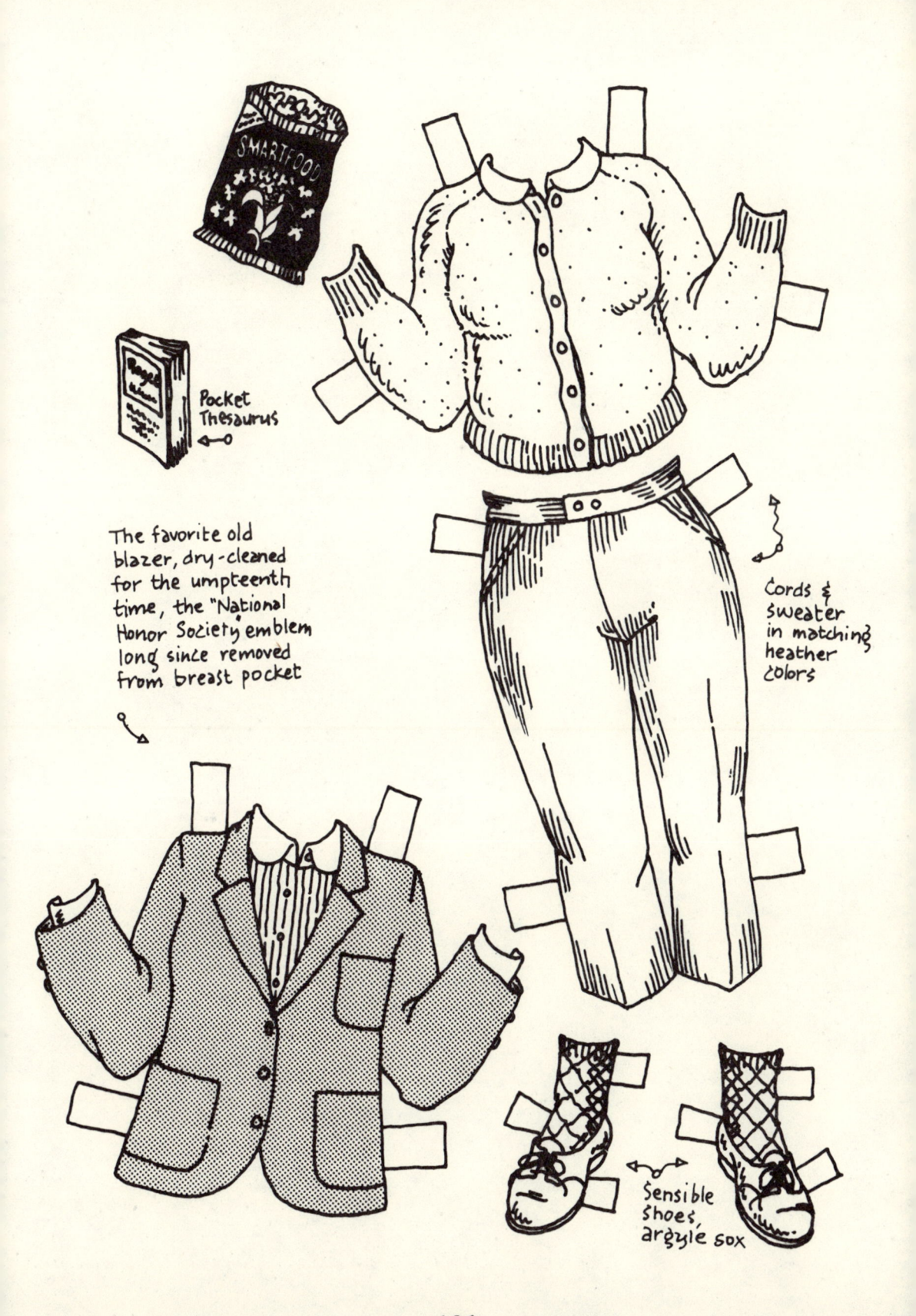

The favorite old blazer, dry-cleaned for the umpteenth time, the "National Honor Society" emblem long since removed from breast pocket

Cords & sweater in matching heather colors

Sensible shoes, argyle sox

Connect the Dyke answers

1) **Identification:** H - Spacey Stacey or Born-Again Pagan

2) **Description:** G - Loose-fitting clothes (so as not to impede the flow of spiritual energy) and a proliferation of crystals hanging from various parts of her body are characteristics of this lesbian. Her clothes mirror her eclectic spiritual practice: multicolored silk pants from Africa, a large bandana in imitation of an Indian serape for a top, and a turban (just for the impact). She is easily recognized by her starry-eyed expression, an aura of serenity, and a perpetual "OM" on her lips.

3) **Accoutrements:** C - Incense, feathers, and an amulet filled with special crystals and stones.

4) **Habitat:** H - Her habitat includes metaphysical bookstores, retreats, and workshops entitled How To Be A Channel Of Love For The Universe While Attaining Personal and Planetary Prosperity.

5) **Transportation:** G - She levitates.

6) **Common expressions:** H - Besides her Mantra she often can be heard uttering phrases like, "Mercury is in retrograde, that's why I'm screwing up. I love your crown chakra halo."

7) **Last book read:** D - Any book by Shirley MacLaine

8) **Heroine:** A - Shirely MacLaine

9) **Social group or professional affiliation:** D - A member of any group exploring whatever metaphysical topic is currently in vogue.

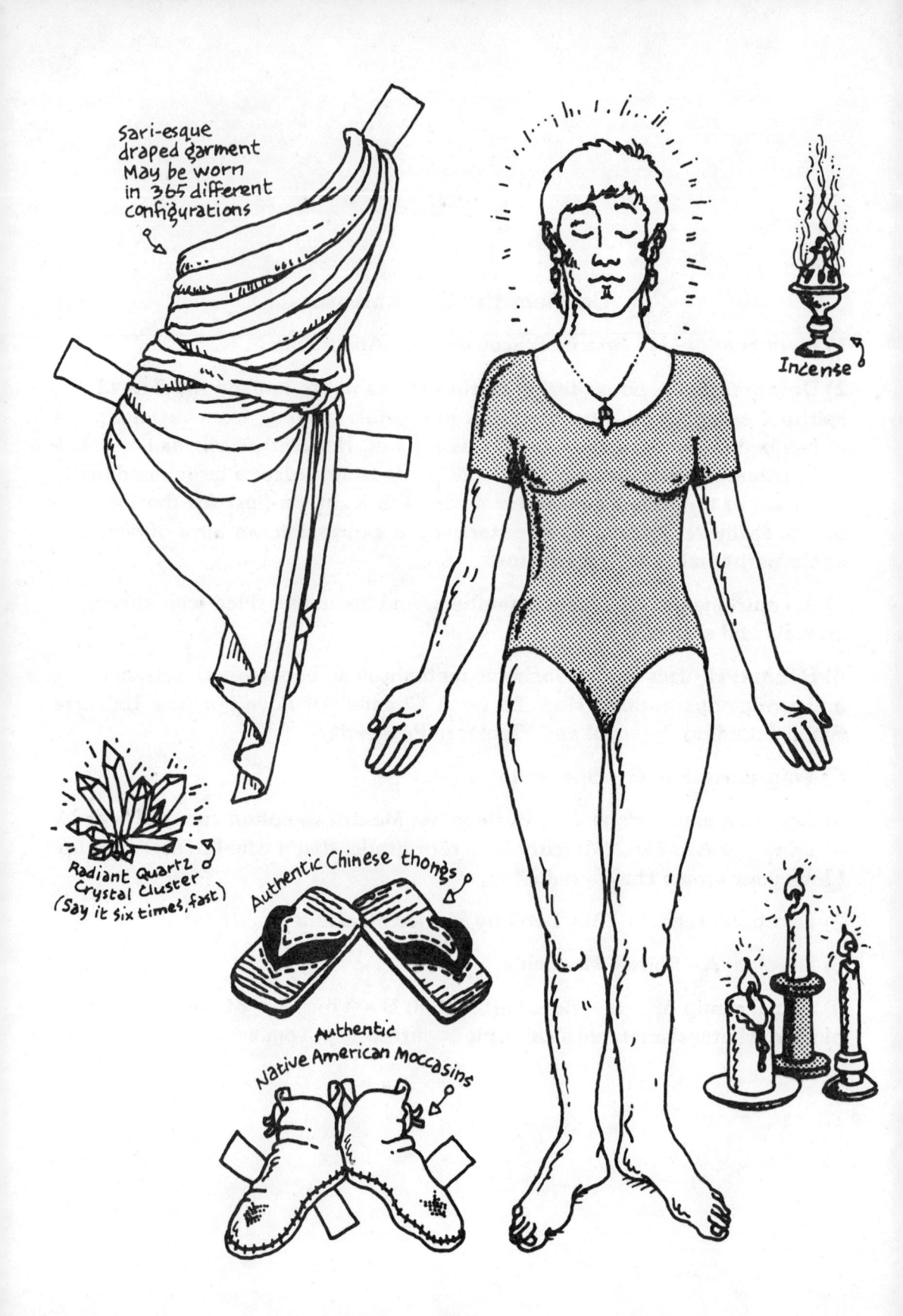

Sari-esque draped garment May be worn in 365 different configurations

Incense

Radiant Quartz Crystal Cluster (Say it six times, fast)

Authentic Chinese thongs

Authentic Native American Moccasins

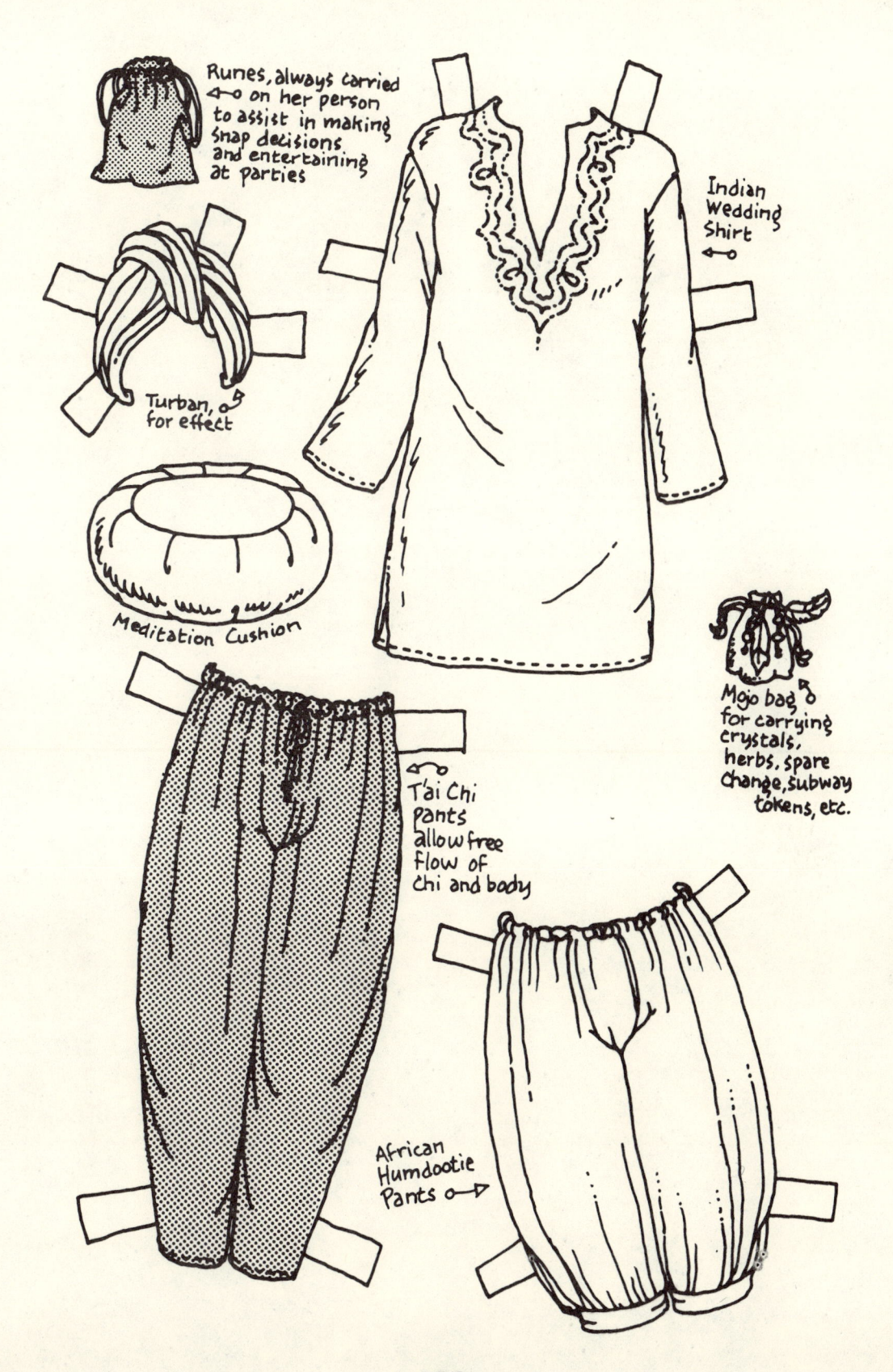

Runes, always carried on her person to assist in making snap decisions and entertaining at parties

Indian Wedding Shirt

Turban, for effect

Meditation Cushion

Mojo bag, for carrying crystals, herbs, spare change, subway tokens, etc.

T'ai Chi pants allow free flow of chi and body

African Humdootie Pants

Connect the Dyke answers

1) Identification: B - Jock

2) Description: F - She wears her hair short so that she can always keep her eye on the ball. She is ready for action in her muscle-revealing tight tee-shirt tucked into her fashionable sweat pants. She is usually wearing white sweat socks in her all-purpose cleats. With a happily competitive outlook, she's up for any game anytime.

3) Accoutrements: D - Softball glove, bat, or any sports equipment in season

4 Habitat: A - Softball fields, basketball courts, golf courses, tennis courts, and grouped en masse in front of any televised sporting event

5) Transportation: E - Small station wagon, large enough to carry athletic gear, yet compact enough to look sporty

6) Common expressions: D - "Diamonds are a girl's best friend."

7) Last book read: B - She rarely reads and when she does it is exclusively about sports; athletes' autobiographies, the sports pages of the newspaper and sports listings in the *TV Guide*.

8) Heroine: D - Martina, Nancy Leiberman, Billie Jean King, and her high school gym teacher

9) Social group or professional affiliation: H - Softball teams, hockey teams, basketball teams, touch football teams, and, when desperate, golf and bowling leagues

← Our heroine plays a mean shortstop

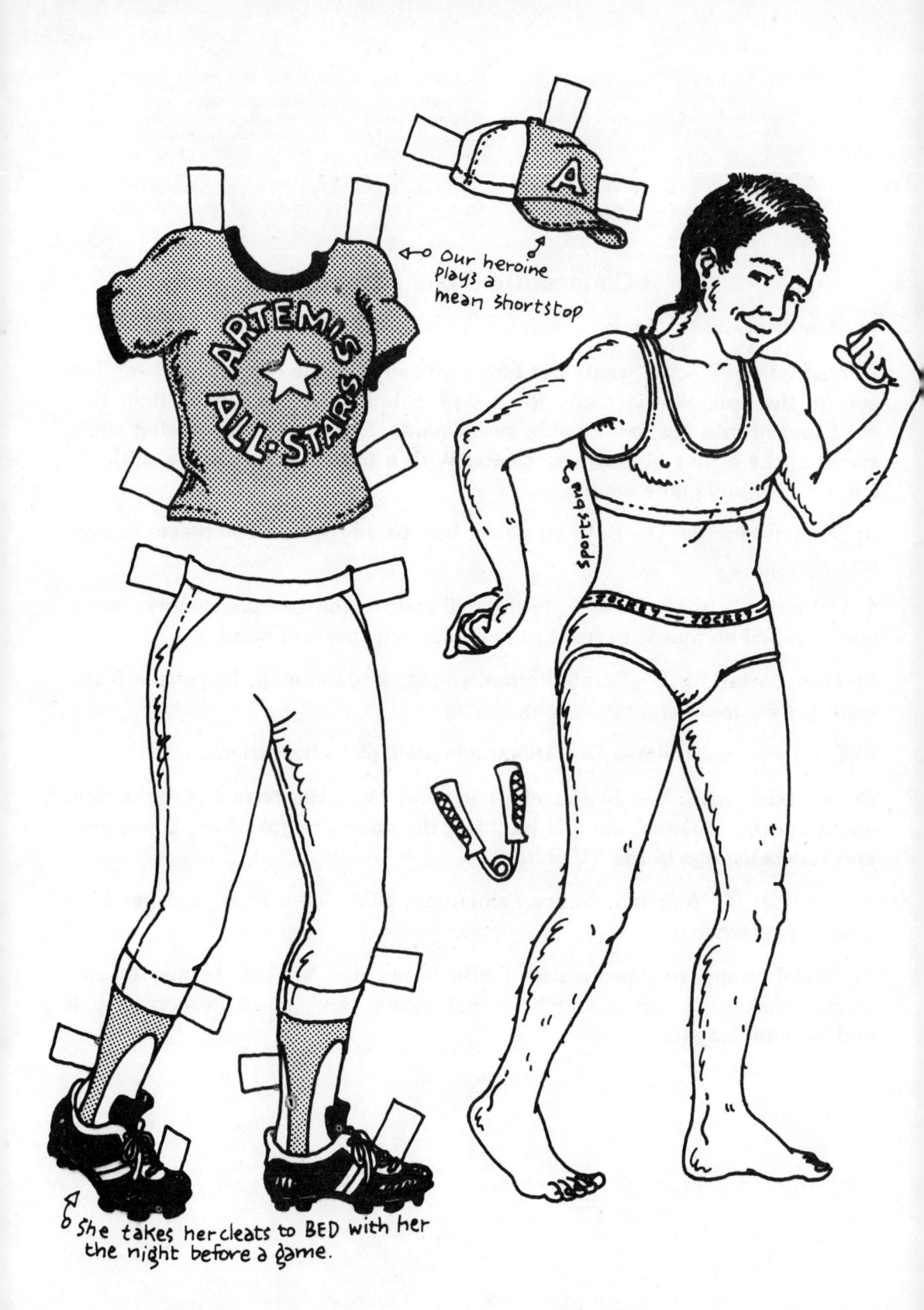

sports bra

She takes her cleats to BED with her the night before a game.

108

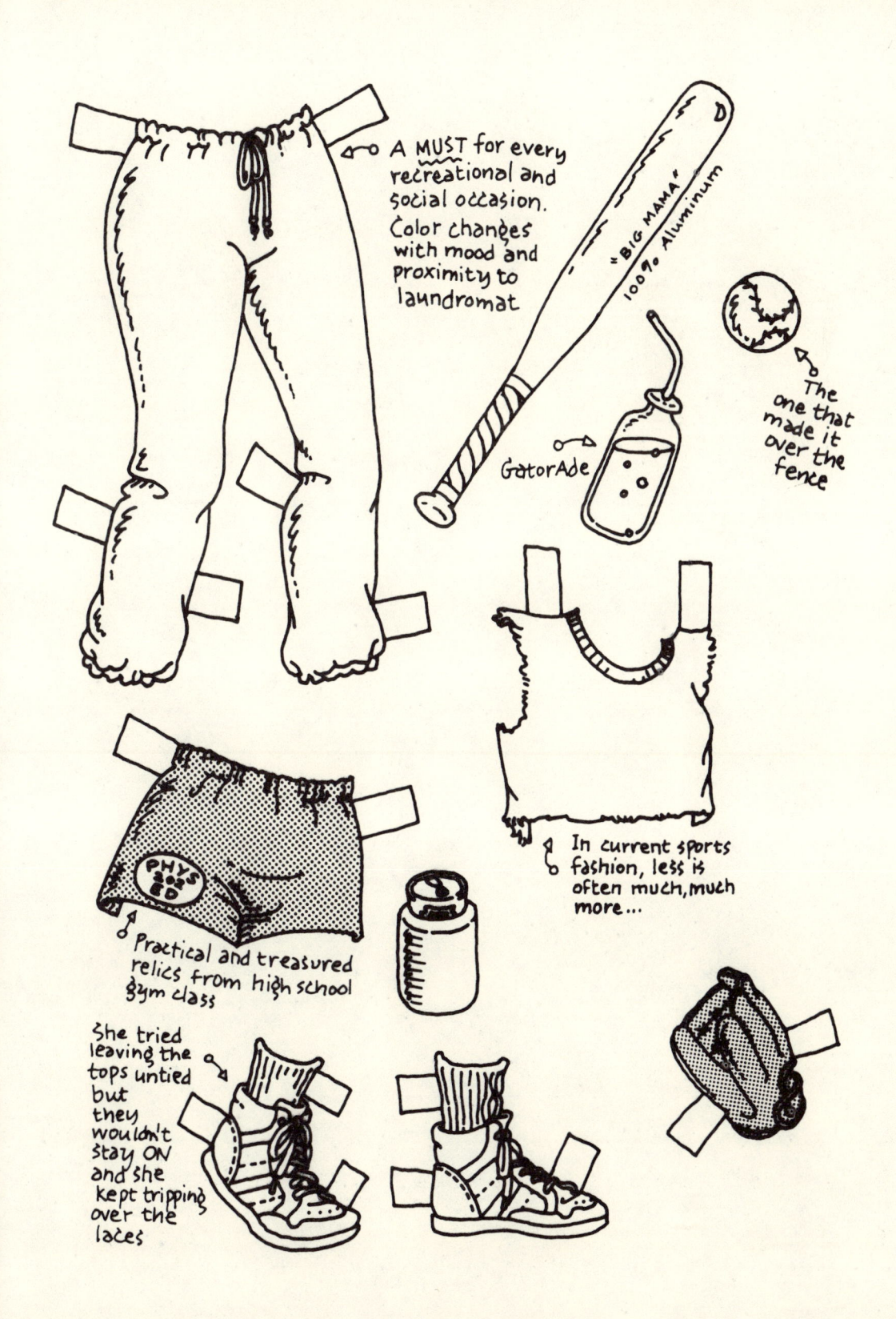

A MUST for every recreational and social occasion. Color changes with mood and proximity to laundromat.

"BIG MAMA" 100% Aluminum

GatorAde

The one that made it over the fence

In current sports fashion, less is often much, much more...

PHYS ED

Practical and treasured relics from high school gym class

She tried leaving the tops untied but they wouldn't stay ON and she kept tripping over the laces

109

Connect the Dyke answers

1) **Identification:** G - Earth Crunchy

2) **Description:** C - She wears her hair long and braided because it would be unnatural to cut it. She has an Ivory Girl face, complete with clear skin and big eyes that take in everything. This lesbian marches to the beat of a different drummer, usually a slow one. Everything, including speech, is slowly and carefully considered. She wears all-natural fibers, from her cotton shirt and denim overalls to her woolen socks slipped into leather clogs.

3) **Accoutrements:** E - She is often seen reaching for GORP (grains, oats, raisins, and peanuts) in her pocket and usually carries around a cup of hot herbal tea.

4) **Habitat:** B - This type of lesbian used to be found almost exclusively at John Denver concerts but now she is everywhere: gardens, camping areas, health food stores, weaving classes, and massage centers.

5) **Transportation:** F - An old VW Squareback, large enough to carry camping or gardening gear or for sleeping in while traveling.

6) **Common expressions:** A - "Would you like some more herbal tea?" "What was I saying?"

7) **Last book read:** G - The *Foxfire* books, and the *Whole Earth Catalogues;* it is possible she has read J.R.R. Tolkien's trilogy again.

8) **Heroine:** C - Adelle Davis

9) **Social group or professional affiliation:** C - Food co-ops, clothing co-ops communal gardens, shared homes, covens, and country dances.

← 100% cotton

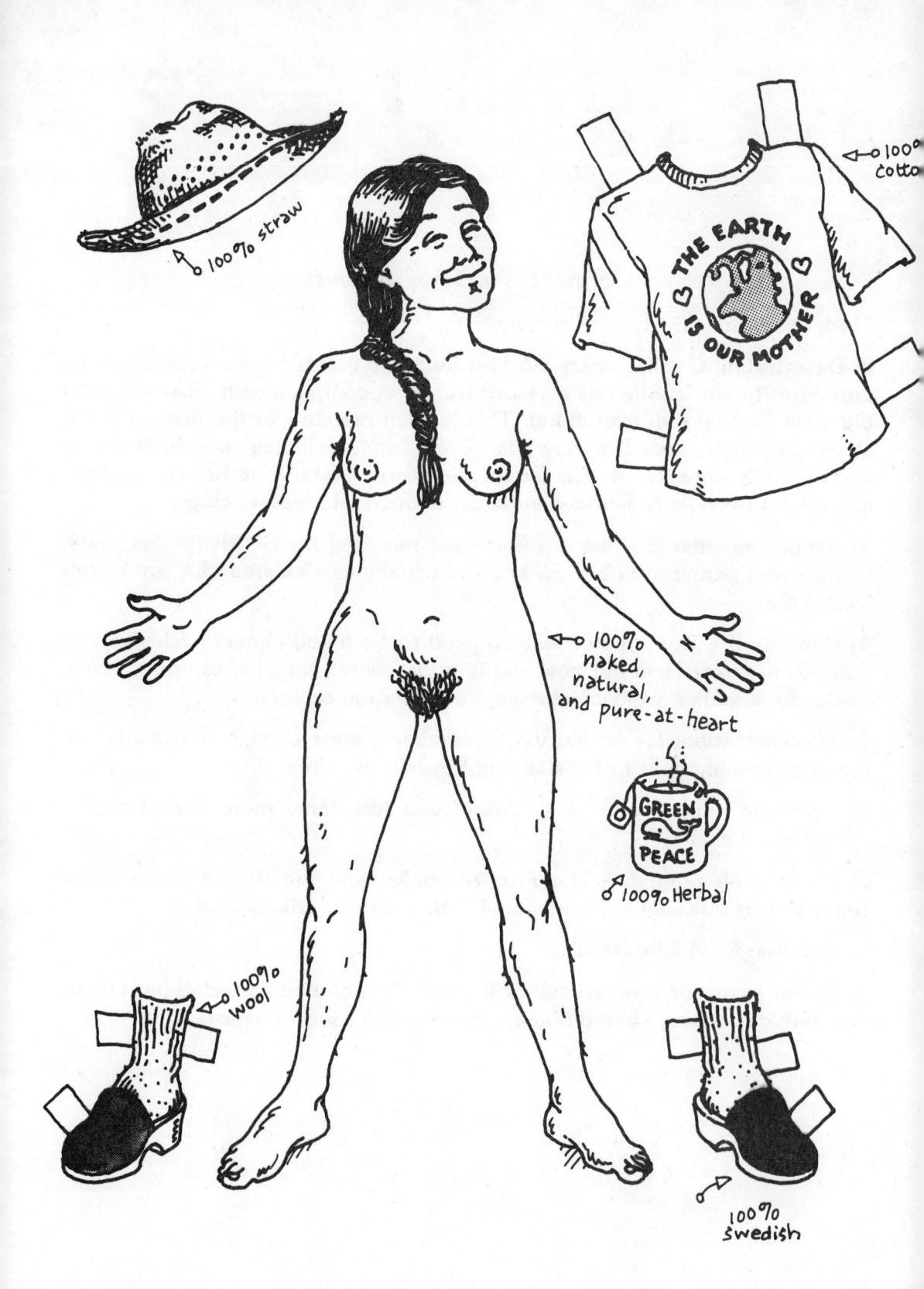

← 100% straw

THE EARTH IS OUR MOTHER

← 100% naked, natural, and pure-at-heart

GREEN PEACE

♂ 100% Herbal

← 100% wool

→ 100% Swedish

112

100% ZIP-LOC baggie of 100% G.O.R.P.

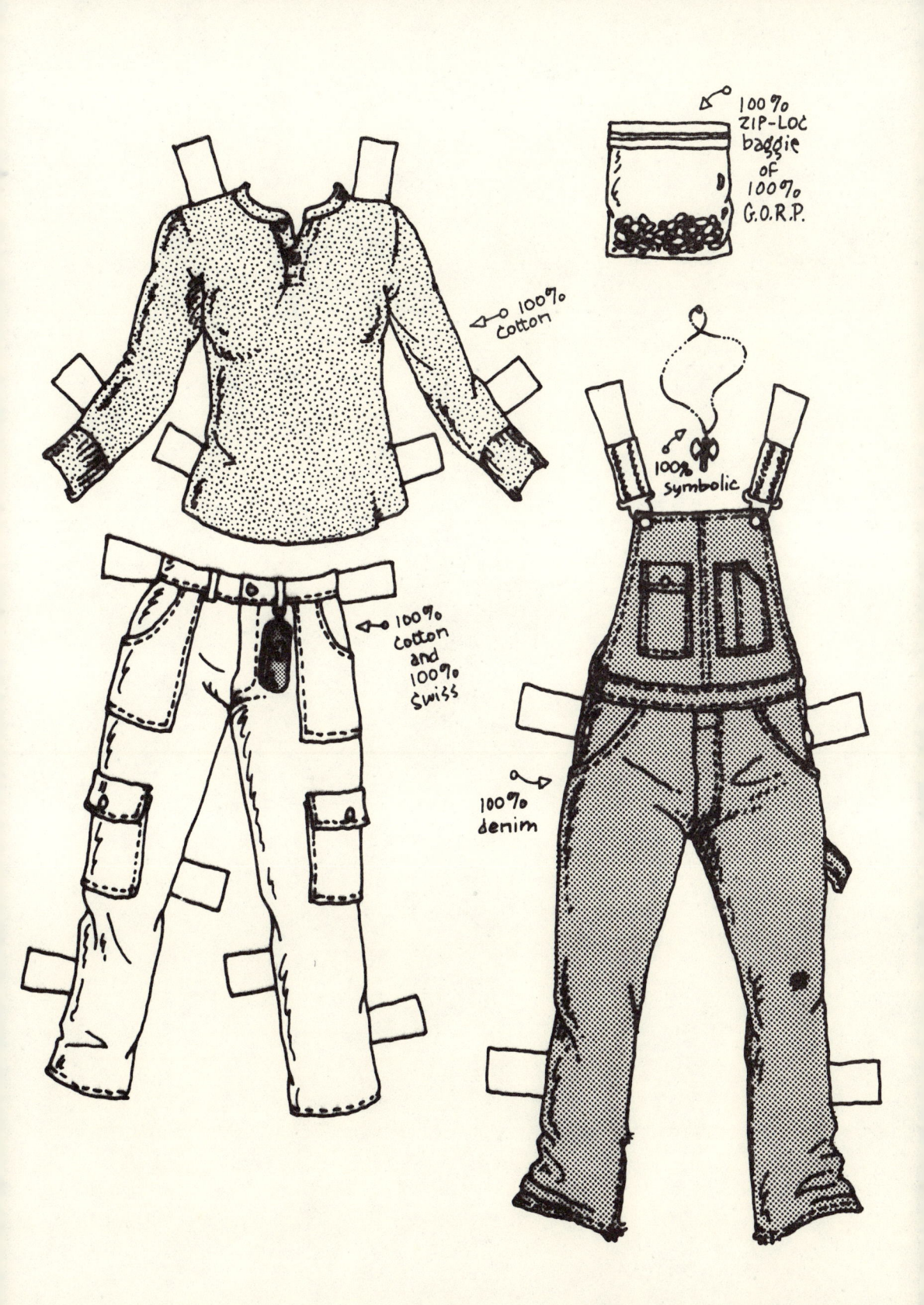

100% cotton

100% Symbolic

100% cotton and 100% Swiss

100% denim

Answers

GIRL GROUPS

Leader of the Pack	Shangri-Las
My Boyfriend's Back	The Angels
Sure the Boy I Love	The Crystals
My Guy	Mary Wells
Soldier Boy	The Shirelles
He's a Fool	Lesley Gore
Then He Kissed Me	The Crystals
Proud Mary	Tina Turner
Johnny Angel	Shelley Fabares
Bobby's Girl	Marcie Blaine
It's in His Kiss	Betty Everett
Johnny Get Angry	Joanie Sommers
Kind of Boy You Can't Forget	Raindrops
Sally Go Round the Roses	The Jaynetts
He's So Fine	Chiffons
I Will Follow Him	Peggy March
Judy's Turn to Cry	Lesley Gore
Please Mr. Postman	The Marvelettes
I Wanna Love Him So Bad	Jelly Beans
He's a Rebel	The Crystals

Classic vowels

Beebo Brinker—Ann Bannon
Rubyfruit Jungle—Rita Mae Brown
The Ladies—Doris Grumbach
Patience and Sarah—Isabel Miller
Well of Loneliness—Radclyffe Hall
Sita—Kate Millet
Choices—Nancy Toder
Desert of the Heart—Jane Rule

What's wrong with this picture?

The leaves of the rose should be on the other side of the blossom when it is reflected in the mirror.

To a Tee

1. "You're out!"
2. overthrow
3. bat (or out)
4. steal
5. "Batter up."
6. strike
7. batting order (batting glove)
8. first base
9. center field
10. bunt
11. home plate
12. triple
13. cleats
14. left field
15. pitcher (or catcher)
16. outfield
17. out (or bat)
18. team
19. water girl
20. short stop
21. catcher (or pitcher)

ACROSTICS

#1
WOODHULL
NIGHTENGALE
BARBARA
JOAN OF ARC
AMELIA
SOJOURNER
STEINEM
FOSSEY

#2
SAPPHO
SACAJAWEA
BARNEY
CHRISTINA
BETHUNE
BOADICEA
DEBORAH
BONNEY

#3
WILMA
JOYNER
LIEBERMAN
BILLIE JEAN
NYAD
EVANS
DIDRIKSON
PATRICE
JOAN
MARTINA
BENOIT
SONJA

#4
HYPATIA
DAVID-NEEL
GOODALL
ANNIE
CATHER
BERYL
CURIE
SALLY

#5
DEMETER
AMAZONS
ARTEMIS
CLEOPATRA
TIBET
KALI
LABRYS
SENECA
HORSE
DYAK

JUMBLES

1 toilet, violin, brooks, grading: GOOD VIBRATIONS!
2 excitedly, media, examples, jetty: MEET MY EX'S EX
3 uncle, moist, crispy, teach: IN THE CLOSET
4 ability, fragile, emulates, nebulus: LESBIAN FEMALE
5 brave, demon, under, float: EAT AND RUN
6 gripe, towers, throttle, gusting: TOUGH TITTIES
7 juries, baby, yearns, treasure: "JUST SAY YES!"
8 maybe, prams, backache, tuned: BUMP, SET, DYKE

Not so Trivia answers:

1. Jill Johnston
2. Monique Wittig
3. Natalie Barney
4. Robin Morgan
5. June Arnold and Parke Bowman
6. *Ruby Fruit Jungle*
7. Barbara Deming
8. *The Ladder*
9. Patrice Donnely
10. Vita Sackville West
11. euphemism for lesbian sexuality
12. yes
13. Florence Kennedy
14. Judy Grahn
15. either from the expression *to be dyked out*, (ie. dressed up) or from Boadicea (a British queen who led a revolt against the Romans)
16. Natalie Barney
17. Valeri Solanis
18. Gloria Steinem
19. Meg Christian
20. Barbara Grier
21. 15: one to write about it for the newsletter, two to argue that natural candlelight is better, three to discuss the nuclear power issue, four to debate putting in a dimmer switch, and five to be supportive.
(Did we forget someone?)

Word Search Answers

(Word search answer grids for puzzles titled: ANDY'S, CHANGES, WOMEN, SEX, and MORE SEX)

Answers

Crystal Clear
1 Ruby
2 Amber
3 Fossil
4 Sunstone
5 Peridot
6 Carnelian

More Crystal Clear
1 Amazonite
2 Fluorite
3 Lapis lazuli
4 Rhodocrosite
5 Sapphire
6 Tourmaline

Sister Colleges
1 Vassar
2 Bryn Mawr
3 Wellesley
4 Mount Holyoke
5 Radcliffe
6 Barnard

Women of the 70s
1 Greer (Germaine)
2 Johnston (Jill)
3 Trilling (Diana)
4 Smeal (Eleanor)
5 Abzug (Bella)
6 Steinem (Gloria)

More Women of the 70s
1 Sloan
2 Reddy (Helen)
3 Rich (Adrienne)
4 Bryant (Anita)
5 Dworkin (Andrea)
6 Kennedy (Florence)

Crossword Answers

#1 Crossword— and Romance

[crossword grid with answers including: L FORM B S LIPSMACK / I N ORGASM A E FUN / BED U O EBB X ANA / HEIT NAP T I ETC / R S D MASSAGES N K / ADILDO A SO E ARC / N R FIG TWOPLAY HOT / GAEA U S E L K O / C EXPERIMENTATION / LIVEN O S AR S G / I SUITSEROS IRIS U / TEATS R U B E / O B ENJOY R U ACTS / RELAX E T END N U / I E VAGINAOILINGS / ASS N R C S SIP U / T GENITALS AMAP C / LOBE ET R A L LICK / PET U STIMULATE]

#2 Crossword—Words of Laughter

[crossword grid with answers including: BUN DANCE BOSOM / A IF U L A E E CAT / LACEY N BISEXUAL 2 / L EM U BIKE D BIT / G H I U E S BOP / DYKE R TANKTOP A P / M G C Y U A BREW / T SIGH L DEGAY R / SEASON COME E A / AMOS H NET CRUSH / COW UP T N E S / HONEYMOONPERIOD I / TEN A T A P HOSE / R T LIPS S TENT / E WAIT U O L R / A I N C EXLOVERSOO / T M G K X W I R / O MOIST T A CANOES / U O NURTURING G W / TON NY A DONT]

#3 Entertainment

[crossword grid with answers including: ROCK JANECHAMBERS S / FEAR LA O DELVE IT / ACTIT OLIVIA TUES A / DO BAD LENT HEATHER / EAR P T R O R A / DESERTHEARTED DRILL / N O HI Y EAR I / KATHERINEHEPBURN EL / A C S G E U B L / THANKS COMEDIAN BALL / E SI ERA O C MARIA / C PLOT L U WATER BEN / LEE TOMLIN R A / I N OH E TRETFURE / N REACTSTO SEE A / TU N A A SARAH T / O FOOTLIGHTS H I U / NEED R I Y ANORGAN / E MEGCHRISTIAN B E / BILL SO ENTIRE YES]

Numberless Answers

#1 Meeting Places

Solved crossword containing: WORKCAMP, BARS, CONCERT, FIRE, NAPLES, LAKE, PARTY, SEA, INNS, COFFEEHOUSES, NOW CAFE, BARN, DISCOS, CAR, GUESTHOUSES, JOBS, CRUISE, SPORTS, LESBIAN GROUP.

#2 F Words

Solved crossword containing: FROLIC, FLUFF, FRIG, WELD, FRENETIC, FANTASY, FAINT, FEMME, FREAK, FLAUNT, FRILLY, FLINCH, FIST, FILE, FINGER, FEEL, FLOW, FRIGGA, FENCE, FREE, FAR, FAN, FRICTION, FAY, FUMBLE, FRENCH.

#3 Politics

Solved crossword containing: LESBIAN AND GAY RIGHTS, WAR, ERA, BOMBS, RACISM, TIMES, ABORTION, TAX, RULE, RIGHT, CLASSISM, BLACK, CHICANA, ABUSE, BILL, CON, PRIVILEGE, PRIDE, CAMPAIGN, HOMELESS, ENABLE.

#4 Hotspots

Solved crossword containing: LONDON, TOPEKA, CANADA, BI, AUSTIN, EUGENE, PROVINCETOWN, FARGO, DENVER, DALLAS, ST LOUIS, PHOENIX.

#5 Counseling

Solved crossword containing: TRAUMA, ALCOHOL, RACE, RELATIONSHIPS, PHOBIA, PRIDE, GROWTH, EX, ABUSE, NO, AGE, STRESS, GRIEFWORK, PAIN, CAREER, SEXUALITY, MEN, FAT, GAY, CONTROL, IDENTITY, FEARS, SANE.

#6 Writers

Solved crossword containing: VITA SACKVILLE WEST, PHRASES, EROTICISM, BOOK, RADCLYFFE HALL, ACT, PHRASE, KNOWS, NAIAD, VIRGINIA WOOLF, JANE RULE, POETRY, IMAGE, MAC, DRAMA, DYKE REACTION, WORD, ROLE, COLON, PRONOUN.

Complaint Department

If you as a _____ Lesbian (s) or a Lesbian (s) of _____ extraction, who is (are) into _____, feel discrimintated against, or, at the very least, feel under represented or over represented in this book, please check the appropriate box (es) or list your own concerns and send this form back to New Victoria Publishers, PO Box 27 Norwich, Vermont 05055 so that we can make *Cutups Two* as politically correct as possible.

☐ This book is sexist.
☐ This book discriminates against homeless dykes.
☐ Most lesbians have more important things to do with their time than cut out paper dolls.
☐ Where is the leather dyke?
☐ Bisexuals have once again been completely ignored by the Lesbian community.
☐ This book is not representative of ethnic minorities.

☐ Dyak	☐ Amerindian	☐ Black
☐ Hispanic	☐ Eskimo	☐ Icelandic
☐ Amazon	☐ Filipina	☐ Sufi
☐ Other_____		

☐ As usual, there are no images of differently-abled Lesbians.
☐ This book ignores the issue of _____ abuse.
☐ The order of these questions is unfair to_____.
☐ These questions have left out_____.
☐ This questionnaire is_____.
☐ This questionnaire should be: ☐ recycled ☐ burned ☐ buried
☐ Other_____
☐ Where is Fifi La Femme?

Here is a space for you to tell us your feelings. What would you have put in this book? In this questionnaire?

Other Titles Available

The Names of the Moons of Mars by Patricia Roth Schwartz ($8.95) In these stories the author writes humorously as well as poignantly about our lives as women and as lesbians.

Found Goddesses: Asphalta to Viscera by Morgan Grey and Julia Penelope ($7.95) *Found Goddesses is wonderful! All of it's funny and some of it's inspired. I've had more fun reading it than any book in the last two years* — Joanna Russ

As The Road Curves by Elizabeth Dean ($8.95) Ramsey had it all; a great job at a prestigious lesbian magazine, and a reputation of never having to sleep alone. Now she takes off on an adventure of a lifetime.

All Out by Judith Alguire ($8.95) Winning a gold medal at the Olympics is Kay Strachan's all-consuming goal. Kay remains determined, until a budding romance with a policewoman threatens her ability to go all out for the gold.

Lesbian Stages by Sarah Dreher ($9.95) *Sarah Dreher's play scripts are treasures: good yarns firmly centered in a Lesbian perspective, peopled with specific, complex, often contadictory—just like real people—characters.* —Kate McDermott

Gray Magic by Sarah Dreher ($8.95) A peaceful vacation with Stoner's friend Stell turns frightening when Stell falls ill with a mysterious disease and Stoner finds herself an unwitting combatant in the great struggle between the Hopi Spirits of good and evil.

Stoner McTavish by Sarah Dreher ($7.95) The original Stoner McTavish mystery introduces psychic Aunt Hermione, practical partner Marylou, and Stoner herself, who goes off to the Grand Tetons to rescue dream lover Gwen.

Something Shady by Sarah Dreher ($8.95) Travel Agent/Detective Stoner McTavish travels to the coast of Maine with her lover Gwen and risks becoming an inmate in a suspicious rest home to rescue a missing nurse.

Morgan Calabresé: The Movie by N. Leigh Dunlap ($5.95) Wonderfully funny comic strips. Politics, relationships, life's changes, and softball as seen through the eyes of Morgan Calabresé.

Look Under the Hawthorn by Ellen Frye ($7.95) A stonedyke from the mountains of Vermont, Edie Cafferty sets off to search for her long lost daughter and, on the way, meets Anabelle, an unpredictable jazz pianist looking for her birth mother.

Runway at Eland Springs by ReBecca Béguin ($7.95) When Anna flying supplies and people into the African bush, finds herself in conflict over her agreement to scout and fly for a game hunter, she turns to Jilu, the woman running a safari camp at Eland Springs, for love and support.

Promise of the Rose Stone by Claudia McKay ($7.95) Mountain warrior Isa goes to the Federation to confront its rulers for her people. She is banished to the women's compound in the living satellite, Olyeve, where she and her lover, Cleothe, plan an escape.

Order from New Victoria Publishers, P.O. Box 27, Norwich, Vt. 05055